W9-BJQ-881

THE PATTEN LECTURES · 1949 · INDIANA UNIVERSITY

Science and English Poetry

A HISTORICAL SKETCH, 1590-1950

BY DOUGLAS BUSH

OXFORD UNIVERSITY PRESS

LONDON   OXFORD   NEW YORK

COPYRIGHT 1950 BY INDIANA UNIVERSITY
FIRST PUBLISHED BY OXFORD UNIVERSITY PRESS, NEW YORK, 1950
FIRST ISSUED AS AN OXFORD UNIVERSITY PRESS PAPERBACK, 1967

THE PATTEN FOUNDATION

Mr. Will Patten of Indianapolis (A.B., Indiana University, 1893) made in 1931 a gift for the establishment of the Patten Foundation at his Alma Mater. Under the terms of this gift, which became available upon the death of Mr. Patten (3 May 1936), there is to be chosen each year a Visiting Professor who is to be in residence several weeks during the year. The purpose of this prescription is to provide an opportunity for members and friends of the University to enjoy the privilege and advantage of personal acquaintance with the Visiting Professor. The Visiting Professor for the Patten Foundation in 1948-9 was Douglas Bush.

PR508 S3 B8

PRINTED IN THE UNITED STATES OF AMERICA

PREFACE: 1950

I need not anticipate here the apologies made in the opening pages for an inevitably sketchy and simple account of a very large and complex subject. It may be said, however, that the isolating of one theme is not meant to suggest that science is the cause of all the troubles of the modern world. While it is a cliché that *homo faber,* the technician, has got out of control, the real cause of our troubles, as poets know, lies within the individual *homo sapiens.*

I was, and remain, happily conscious of the honor of being invited to lecture on the Patten Foundation at Indiana University. And it is very pleasant to recall both the staunchness of the audience and the abundant and cordial hospitality that my wife and I received from the academic community during a six-week visit. In particular I am grateful to Professor Ralph E. Cleland, chairman of the committee on the Patten lectureship, for his unfailing kindness in many matters large and small.

The history of these discourses, while hardly momentous in itself, calls up other pleasant memories. The subject was first discussed at large in two lectures at Victoria College in the University of Toronto. Single lectures from the Patten series were given (with the ready consent of the Foundation) at the New England Renaissance Conference at Connecticut College, the University of Illinois, Butler University, the

Indiana State Teachers College at Terre Haute, Syracuse University, and the College Club of Boston; and several were given during an enjoyable week spent at Emory University and Agnes Scott College. To my generous hosts and hearers at these institutions I return thanks.

After laboring mightily at a bibliography that would add ballast to a little craft that carries too much sail for its size, I found that the effect would be to sink it; and that, moreover, since the subject has no limits, even the longest list would remain quite inadequate and arbitrary. That and incessant references being alike impossible, I can make only a general acknowledgment of my obligations to a multitude of books and articles. But I must thank Professor F. E. L. Priestley for his reply to a query growing out of his valuable article, 'Newton and the Romantic Concept of Nature,' which appeared in the *University of Toronto Quarterly* in 1948; and Mr. John L. Sweeney for reading, in only too amiable a spirit, my discourse on modern poetry (he is not of course responsible for my errors or blind spots).

Douglas Bush

March 1950
Cambridge, Massachusetts

PREFACE: 1967

Since this small book first appeared in 1950, both pure science and technology have made still greater advances on all fronts, from the further conquest of disease to the further conquest of outer space. Thus science has become more firmly established than ever as the dominant power in our civilization, the governing and directing authority to which all else must bow—except perhaps human passions. It is no less obvious that, as Tennyson said, 'Knowledge comes, but wisdom lingers,' and, when we survey the general state of our world, it appears that various kinds of unwisdom and violence are impeding our arrival at the millennium. Indeed, while the non-scientific layman may rejoice in manifold scientific achievements, he may also be shocked by doctrines put forth by some ultra-modern minds: for example, that, because science is increasingly able to control man's environment or, through appropriate drugs or brain-washing, to alter his very nature, there is less and less need for the virtues supposedly nourished by the humanities, so that we may look forward happily to a world in which there will be no more intellectual or moral struggle. To many people this utopian vision is not of life but of death. Such scientific spectres may remain spectres, or they may be translated into the concrete terms of the almighty computer; at any rate their sinister presence has grown more and more oppressive. A great deal of modern writing has been a direct or indirect protest against the dehumanizing of man, against his being reduced to mechanical dimensions, to a statistical cipher. While science has brought momentous discoveries and benefits, there has been also a growing conviction—which has contributed to our general unrest— that science and technology have brought *homo sapiens* to the point of diminishing returns. If to some minds poetry, in such a world, appears as an anachronism, to others it may appear more than ever an urgent necessity as an assertion of individual human experience, of the validity of the artist's vision of life.

All this, to be sure, may sound portentous and pretentious in relation to what is—though based on several hundred books and articles—the merest sketch of successive periods of co-existence or conflict; but, whatever the sketchiness of the book, its theme is fundamental and has infinite ramifications. In looking over these pages again, I think that, so far as my knowledge goes, the general picture remains true. (To squeeze in an unphilosophical footnote, the airy navies of *Locksley Hall,* mentioned on page 162, were apparently balloons, not airplanes.) In the nature of the case, the chapter on modern poetry is most subject to our changing perspective and may be modified in various ways by readers more expert than I. Since the late Aldous Huxley appears briefly in that chapter, I might mention his last book, *Literature and Science* (1963), which seemed a rather odd valedictory from the author of *Brave New World* (1932). Rebuking modern poets for their failure to grasp and use the ideas and images of science, Huxley pointed out the fallacious responses of Keats, Arnold, and Eliot to the nightingale's song: these poets did not know that the bird sings only to warn its neighbors that it is staking out a time and place for the consumption of caterpillars. This example of unscientific error would not appear to strengthen Huxley's general thesis.

It is pleasant to have my small book given a new lease of life.

In ushering it into its new home I have taken occasion to glance over the many reviews of the first edition. Almost all of them were more or less cordial. J. R. Newman gave the book a lavish spread in *The Scientific American*. A distinguished English scientist, E. N. da C. Andrade, liked the book well enough to review it in two periodicals. One literary reviewer took me to task—this is a common line with reviewers in general—for not having written a different kind of book, on the poetic use of scientific imagery (I had said at the start that I was concerned with the history of ideas and must treat poems as documents). The same possibility was suggested by another man of letters, who observed incidentally that I cared 'only for poetry written on the basis of man's guilt and his knowledge of the Fall'—a revelation of my taste possibly correct but quite new to me. Two or three reviewers denied any conflict between science and poetry, but for opposite reasons—that the two activities belong to the same imaginative quest, and that they belong to the qualitatively different domains of knowledge and value. Whether we like it or not, it would appear that there is now, even if there was not in some earlier periods, an inescapable gap or conflict between the nature and claims of science and the nature and claims of poetry, that the scientific and positivist insistence on one sole kind of 'truth' inevitably makes poetry something other and decidedly less than truth. If scientists (and social scientists) are now the not unacknowledged legislators of the world, there are, outside the legislative 'corridors of power,' a goodly number of articulate persons who remain stubbornly averse to being scientifically processed and stubbornly determined to live and feel and think and suffer as individual human beings.

May 1967   D. B.
Cambridge, Massachusetts

ACKNOWLEDGMENTS

For permission to quote from copyright books I am indebted to the following publishers:

Cornell University Press, for the quotation from Horace M. Kallen, *The Liberal Spirit;*

Harcourt, Brace & World, Inc., and Faber and Faber, Ltd., for quotations from T. S. Eliot, *Collected Poems;*

Harper & Brothers and Chatto and Windus, for the quotation from Aldous Huxley, *Leda and Other Poems;*

Harvard University Press, for the quotation from Douglas Bush, *Mythology and the Romantic Tradition in English Poetry;*

Holt, Rinehart and Winston, Inc., and Jonathan Cape, Ltd., for the quotation from Robert Frost, *Collected Poems;*

The Macmillan Company, Mr. M. B. Yeats, the Macmillan Co. of Canada, and Macmillan & Co., Ltd., for quotations from W. B. Yeats, *Collected Poems;*

The Macmillan Company and Macmillan & Co., Ltd., for quotations from Thomas Hardy, *Collected Poems;* and A. N. Whitehead, *Science and the Modern World;*

Macmillan & Co., Ltd., and Mr. Raglan Squire, for the quotation from Sir John Squire, *Collected Poems of Sir John Squire;*

William Morrow & Company and Cassell & Company, for the quotation from Gerald Heard, *The Third Morality;*

Random House, Inc., and Faber and Faber, Ltd., for the quotation from *Collected Poetry of W. H. Auden;*

Charles Scribner's Sons and Constable & Company, for quotations from *Poetical Works of George Meredith;*

Yale University Press and Routledge and Kegan Paul, for the quotation from Geoffrey West, *Charles Darwin;*

and the Executors of the estate of H. G. Wells (Mrs. M. Wells), for the quotation from *Boon.*

D. B.

CONTENTS

I

The Elizabethans: The Medieval Heritage, 3

II

The New Science and the Seventeenth-Century Poets, 27

III

Newtonianism, Rationalism, and Sentimentalism, 51

IV

The Romantic Revolt against Rationalism, 79

V

Evolution and the Victorian Poets, 109

VI

Modern Science and Modern Poetry, 139

CONTENTS

SCIENCE AND ENGLISH POETRY

The Elizabethans: The Medieval Heritage

In this book I shall try to sketch the repercussions of science upon English poetry from the Elizabethan age to the present. The subject is not so clear-cut and straightforward as it might seem to be. It embraces, obviously, the great body of poetry written in the last three and a half centuries, the development of various sciences during the same long period, and the direct response of poets to scientific thought and discovery. That is complex enough. But we are also obviously involved with the history of religion, metaphysics, and ethics and the increasing pressure of science upon traditional orthodoxies; with the growth of our mechanical and industrial civilization and its effects upon the life and spirit of man in general and poets in particular; and with the changes in the technique and texture as well as the content of poetry that have been brought about by the great changes in the poet's outer and inner world. And other related topics might be added.

These headings are large subjects in themselves, and many large books have been written on one or another of their multitudinous aspects. I can only acknowledge a congenital weakness for biting off more than I can chew; I have always had a fellow feeling for a graduate student I once heard of, who proposed doing a thesis on the influence of the eighteenth century on the nineteenth. As we proceed, therefore, I shall doubtless be leaping like a circus rider from horse to horse, or rather, perhaps, be imitating the hero who mounted his horse and rode off in all directions. I do not pretend to be offering any novel ideas, but I hope that, even if the topics discussed are familiar to students of literature and science, there may be some interest in following, however inadequately, a story of prime importance through some three hundred and fifty years. Of course, if we had time, we might go back to Chaucer and beyond, but it is only around 1600 that science begins to shake the faith men live by, and it is poets' reactions to that conflict that will be our main theme. Such a theme requires the use of poetry largely as a series of documents, a procedure that is not approved by critics who are less concerned with what a poet says than with how he says it; I trust, however, that our preoccupation with poets' creeds and philosophies will not seem to imply indifference to the *sine qua non* of poetic power.

Finally, since the nature of the subject focuses attention upon the obverse or destructive side of scientific progress, it might be well to say, once for all, that I am aware that the history of science is a great record of patient search, discovery, and illumination (not to mention its material benefits), and that I am not at any time playing the fatuous role of obscurantist. No one would suggest that certain conceptions of God and man and human life, because they were noble and long-lived, should have been permitted—if that had been possible—to rest on illusion or delusion. In 1664 the Cambridge Platonist, Henry More, one of the first philosophic minds in England to grapple with the problem of science and religion, declared that 'there is no real clashing at all betwixt any genuine point of Christianity and what true philosophy and right reason does determine or allow, but . . . there is a perpetual peace and agreement betwixt truth and truth, be they of what nature or kind so ever.' That there can be no conflict between truth and truth is surely axiomatic in every age. But in every age also there have been, among scientists, religionists, and artists, inevitable errors, uncertainties, and conflicting views of truth, and our journey lies over that darkling plain. One could wish that there were a clear light somewhere ahead of us.

The general problem can be briefly stated. A poet, granted his special endowment, is a person devoted to achieving and expressing a view of human experience, and even that vague and simple definition implies some degree of positive faith in the worth and dignity of life and man. The poet's vision grows out of both his imaginative intuition and his actual experience and knowledge, and knowledge, in the modern centuries, has become increasingly scientific. But science, which is devoted to the discovery of verifiable truth about nature and the means of controlling nature, is not at all concerned about the worth and dignity of life and man—though scientists, as men, may be. It is a commonplace that the effect of science has been to dislodge man from his supposedly central position in a divine order, to reduce him to a dubiously relevant—though unique—accident in an infinite universe and an infinite biological process, and, in recent times, to make him also a victim both of the mechanical forces that he has created and of the blind forces within himself that he has not created. In such a predicament, can man in general, and the artist as the quintessence of man, retain the belief in a supernatural order which all religions have affirmed and which naturalistic science denies? Can he at least continue to sustain himself with the belief that man and life have a dignity and meaning that transcend the chaotic succession of events? He may believe, with the scientist, that the truth shall make you free, but free from what? From error, no doubt, and also, perhaps, from any kind of faith or anchorage whatever. The scientist, setting such questions aside, may find complete spiritual satisfaction in his daily work in the laboratory; but the mass of men, and the poet, have no such alleviation or escape.

Science goes rapidly out of date, great literature is always alive; and some of the fundamental problems are as old as the Old Testament, or older. If the Hebrews attained the highest ancient conception of a providential God, they also put forth the grandest of all questionings of divine order and justice. When the Lord out of the whirlwind rebuked Job for his ignorant presumption and want of faith, he appealed to his own creation and government of the whole world of nature:

Where wast thou when I laid the foundations of the earth? declare, if thou hast understanding.

Who hath laid the measures thereof, if thou knowest? or who hath stretched the line upon it? . . .

Hast thou entered into the springs of the sea? or hast thou walked in the search of the depth?

Have the gates of death been opened unto thee? or hast thou seen the doors of the shadow of death? . . .

Canst thou bind the sweet influences of Pleiades, or loose the bands of Orion? . . .

Canst thou lift up thy voice to the clouds, that abundance of waters may cover thee?

Canst thou send lightnings, that they may go, and say unto thee, Here we are?

Who hath put wisdom in the inward parts? or who hath given understanding to the heart?

The twentieth-century scientist might answer modestly, 'Yes, I can make rain, and I can send something more destructive than lightning,' but the great questions remain questions.

Similar problems, conceived in a more philosophic way, were central in the Greek view of life. Is the race of men, Homer asks, no more than the generation of leaves, or do individual virtue and fortitude have a meaning in a dark world of strife and futility? Sophocles celebrates the inventive skill and prowess of man, who has conquered the beasts and the earth and the sea but cannot conquer death and time; yet he also sees the ephemeral race as guided and bound by the divine laws that never grow old. Some centuries later, Lucretius, with messianic fervor, preaches the science of Epicurean materialism which will free humanity from supernatural dread. And then comes Virgil, envying the man who could plumb the causes of things and tread under foot all fears and inexorable fate and the roar of greedy Acheron; and he arrives at the final vision that Tennyson summed up:

Thou that seëst Universal Nature moved by Universal Mind;
Thou majestic in thy sadness at the doubtful doom of human kind.

As the two Roman names at least remind us, even the special conflict that we are concerned with appeared very early in the history of thought. And long before Lucretius the Greeks had raised the questions of permanence and flux, reality and appearance, nature and convention. Plato, following upon many scientific thinkers and poets, achieved a reconciliation of opposites, a comprehensive orthodoxy that was ethical, metaphysical, and religious. But in Plato's own time, opposed to his central doctrine that God is the measure of all things, there was the doctrine, associated with the Sophist Protagoras, that man is the measure of all things; and we should not forget that other ancient father of modernism, Democritus, who saw the world as composed of atoms and a void. In that antithesis is the essence of all subsequent conflicts. If, according to the late Professor Whitehead, the European philosophical tradition consists of a series of footnotes to Plato, it might be said that the history of skepticism and naturalism is an elaboration of Protagoras and Democritus. But the conflict between those perennial modes of thought did not resume the center of the philosophic stage until the seventeenth century, when the revival of ancient skepticism and naturalism, assisted by some medieval heterodoxies, revived the old opposition in recognizably modern terms. We may remember also that the scientific renaissance of the sixteenth century owed much to the Platonic tradition; and as we go on we shall be observing how, when scientific rationalism becomes mechanistic and inhuman, the same Platonic tradition is a continual source of religious and poetic idealism.

Those things lie ahead. In this first chapter I want to speak, briefly, of four related topics: the 'scientific' notions of the world and man inherited by Shakespeare and other Elizabethans; the religious and philosophic orthodoxy with which those notions were bound up; the Renaissance development of skepticism and naturalism which was beginning to challenge that orthodoxy; and, lastly, the reactions of two or three Elizabethan poets to these early questionings, just before the new science has impressed itself upon the educated consciousness.

Although the year 1543 brought forth the great works of Copernicus and Vesalius, these and other scientific ideas made their way slowly even among the learned, and the Elizabethan view of the world and man remained fundamentally medieval and prescientific. This summary statement (like many other statements in this book) refers of course to the normal, not the exceptional, mind; in the Middle Ages there was far more scientific activity than was suspected two generations ago, and Shakespeare's England contained a number of mathematicians and scientists whose knowledge ranged far beyond the nor-

mal. But at that time, as in our time and in our minds, old
and new ideas existed side by side, and the old greatly pre-
dominated. Of the strong persistence of medievalism, in Europe at large, we have concrete evidence in the printing and
reprinting of such pseudo-scientific encyclopaedias as those
of Isidore of Seville (seventh century) and Bartholomaeus
Anglicus (thirteenth century). An enlarged and not very critical revision of this last was a handbook of Shakespeare's age.
From *Batman upon Bartholome* of 1582 and Burton's *Anatomy of Melancholy*—which agree in many of the items to be
mentioned—one may get a pretty good picture of the stock
of information in the Elizabethan mind. Various works might
of course be drawn upon, such as Sylvester's translation of
Du Bartas' epic of creation, which was among other things
a religious compendium of orthodox science and which remained popular through the first half of the seventeenth
century.

In spite of books written by English Copernicans, the cosmology of Shakespeare and most of his fellows was the Ptolemaic or Aristotelian system, much patched up in the course
of the centuries but still the same in essentials. Around a stationary earth a series of spheres carried the sun and moon and
other planets; outside of these were a varying number of
other spheres, and all were kept in motion by the outermost,
the *primum mobile,* and were presided over, in Neoplatonic
and Christian tradition, by angels. Astrology, whether in ex-
treme or modified forms, was almost universally accepted, and
by some of the chief thinkers of Europe. Even Kepler, the
great lawgiver of astronomy, had mystical notions of the solar
system. Along with astrology went belief in comets, meteors,
and all sorts of unusual phenomena as divine portents. Physical nature and the human body were composed of the four
elements, earth, water, air, and fire, which had the four quali-

ties of heat and cold, dryness and moisture. The body contained four humors, analogous to the elements, namely, blood, phlegm, choler, and melancholy; according as one of these was present in excess, it would cause a sanguine, phlegmatic, choleric, or melancholy temper. The medium between body and soul was spirit. 'Spirit,' says Burton, 'is a most subtle vapor, which is expressed from the blood, and the instrument of the soul, to perform all his actions.' There are three kinds of spirit, natural, vital, and animal, begotten respectively in the liver, the heart, and the brain. The brain, to quote Burton again, 'is a soft, marrowish, and white substance, engendered of the purest part of seed and spirits, included by many skins, and seated within the skull or brain-pan, and it is the most noble organ under heaven, the dwelling-house and seat of the soul, the habitation of wisdom, memory, judgment, reason, and in which man is most like unto God.' (The range of that sentence goes well beyond modern textbooks of physiology or psychology.) 'The common division of the soul is into three principal faculties, vegetal, sensitive, and rational, which make three distinct kind of living creatures, vegetal plants, sensible beasts, rational men.' In such mixtures of classical and medieval ideas, bits of empirical knowledge are elaborated and arranged in symmetrical patterns that are mainly a matter of logical or speculative theory.

The Renaissance man, like the medieval man, saw the natural world in several ways, which could be distinct or could run together. Those ways may be roughly labeled the everyday, the 'scientific,' and the religious. The scientific view has been briefly indicated. By the everyday view I mean that the world of nature was the world that presented itself to the senses and emotions, the familiar world of form and color and creative and destructive energies, not a set of problems to be investigated or of forces to be mastered; and that view

was, until the seventeenth century, largely shared by philosophers. The religious view was more complex. For Aquinas and
for Calvin alike, God revealed himself first through his word
and secondarily through his works; and the unphilosophic
St. Francis could, as one of a great family, praise the Lord
God and all his creatures, our brother the sun and our sister
the moon, our brothers the wind and fire, our sister the water,
our mother the earth.

Of great importance for poetry was a special development
of the religious view of nature and, in some sense, of the
scientific view as well: that was the allegorical or emblematic
conception. Because God maintains an active and intimate
connection with his works, because all creatures and things
and ideas flow from and back to one divine source, there is an
unlimited network of correspondences binding together the
physical and the spiritual, the earthly and the human and
the celestial. Everything, concrete or abstract, is related, directly or by analogy, to everything else. The physical world,
with its rivers and grass, is reflected in the microcosm, man,
with his veins and hair. The basic unity of all things was
presupposed in astrology and alchemy, and that speculative
faith, however unscientific, has been partly realized by modern science. And the medieval or Renaissance man would have
been delighted but hardly surprised by the view, put forth at
one stage in modern physics, that the atom was a sort of
miniature solar system. Because of this general belief in the
divine unity of all creation, natural objects were seen not so
much in themselves but as emblems or allegories of moral,
religious, and metaphysical truth. From this mode of thought
and feeling came the bestiaries, those collections of allegorical
beast-fables and unnatural natural history which included the
phoenix and the unicorn as well as animals known to the zoo.
The same impulse engendered the hundreds of Renaissance

emblem books, which revived this and other kinds of lore in a special literary and pictorial form, and which exerted a strong influence on many poets, such as Spenser, Shakespeare, Chapman, Donne, and George Herbert. Parallel manifestations in other areas were the often complex emblematic codes of graphic art and the allegorizing of pagan fiction, such as Ovid's tales, in terms of Christian truth.

Persons who use the word 'medieval' as a synonym for 'naive' and 'credulous' of course regard all this sort of thing as wild nonsense, and, so far as it purports to be accurate information, no doubt it usually is. But, so far as it touches literature, to dismiss it as unscientific is no wiser than to dismiss a scientist's report of an experiment because it is not poetical. We might remember that this mode of apprehension and expression, on its highest level, produced the *Divine Comedy*. And, in general, we might remember that minds that worked in this allegorical way were not concerned with scientific ends. They were concerned with the religious nature and destiny of man in a divinely ordered world, and their imagination naturally and necessarily made use of more or less religious symbols. In short, the allegorical instinct is closely related to the poetic instinct, since a poet works through metaphor and symbol. If much of the traditional lore of nature that was considered true was not true, the fact of untruth had small bearing on the validity of the symbol. We might remember also that four hundred years after Copernicus we talk of the sunrise and the sunset, and we shall go on doing so; in the age of Einstein we do not make our daily appointments in accordance with the space-time continuum. In other words, our primary experience and responses, which are the main stuff of poetry, are outside the criteria of natural science.

In the Elizabethan age the beginnings of modern science have hardly affected the general consciousness, and the medie-

val ways of looking at the world and man are illustrated everywhere in Shakespeare and his fellows. Physical phenomena,
natural and supernatural, touch human life closely at every
turn. Of Shakespeare's manifold abundance of everyday observation there is no need to speak, and we can only remind
ourselves of some other kinds of knowledge. He was quite indifferent, even in his late plays, to the new astronomy which
was being verified by contemporary scientists. His allusions
to the celestial system are Ptolemaic and astrological and
mythological. Of the many Shakespearian characters who use
astrological terms, nearly all do so as a matter of course; skepticism is expressed by very few—especially, and significantly, by
the naturalistic villain Edmund in *King Lear*. Meteors,
eclipses, and other celestial portents are often accepted, as in
Julius Caesar, and sometimes ridiculed, as in Hotspur's talk
with Glendower. The Pythagorean and Neoplatonic music of
the spheres has its best-known English description in Lorenzo's
moonlight dialogue with Jessica. Like other Elizabethan poets,
Shakespeare draws metaphors from alchemy. From the traditional lore of natural history come the basilisk that kills with
a glance, the chameleon, the salamander, the phoenix, and the
unicorn. Othello tells Desdemona of men whose heads grow
beneath their shoulders. There is much native folklore, especially of the fairies, whom Shakespeare re-created as tiny creatures. There are, on the tragic level, ghosts and evil spirits
and witches. The ghost of Hamlet's father

> faded on the crowing of the cock.
> Some say that ever, 'gainst that season comes
> Wherein our Saviour's birth is celebrated,
> The bird of dawning singeth all night long;
> And then, they say, no spirit dare stir abroad,
> The nights are wholesome, then no planets strike,

No fairy takes, nor witch hath power to charm,
So hallow'd and so gracious is the time.

And Horatio replies, 'So have I heard and do in part believe it.'

How much of these and other popular and learned beliefs Shakespeare actually shared, and how much he used because such things were part of the common consciousness, we cannot be sure; but it is reasonable to assume that he accepted at least a large measure of what his contemporaries accepted. And however we apply that vague criterion, it is plain that he believed many things about the natural world and man that are not so—a fact that is not of the slightest importance. What does matter is that Shakespeare's beliefs and misinformation—including whatever he may have got from treatises on psychology—did not blur but enriched a conception of man as man, as a substantial personality compounded of reason and passion, the divine and the animal, a creature standing or crawling between earth and heaven, whose thoughts and actions are bound up with both natural and supernatural worlds and are weighted with both immediate and eternal significance.

For a fuller realization of that, we may turn to our second topic, the religious and philosophic doctrines with which science was allied. Fundamentalist theology, then as always, made man the center of a stupendous drama. God created the world for man's benefit and happiness, but Adam fell, and his fall necessitated the redemption of the race, through the love and sacrifice of the second Adam. The world is, until the last day, a battleground between God and his good angels and Satan and his evil spirits, who operate through God's permissive will. For one clear example, the damned Macbeth has linked himself with the powers of darkness, and Malcolm, about to lead an army against him, declares: 'The pow'rs above Put on their instruments.' Since God is an active ruler as well as creator, the course of world history, as we see in Sir Walter Ralegh's eloquent work, is a record of divine judgments upon kings and empires. The soul of individual man is likewise a battleground, as the morality plays had pictured it, between the forces of good and evil, and the issue is everlasting bliss or everlasting pain.

In most educated minds this creed had philosophic extensions derived from the classical tradition. The modern phrase 'Christian humanism' sums up the results of the long effort, which began with some of the church fathers and reached its first great synthesis with Aquinas, to reconcile and fuse the natural knowledge and wisdom of the ancient pagans with the supernatural illumination of Christianity. The Renaissance philosophy of order, though not a *Summa* built by any one mind, was a reassertion of the rationality of God and the rational dignity and free will of man—hence, for example, Erasmus' break with Luther and Milton's with Calvinism. This philosophy of order has been rather often discussed of late years and needs no long description here. The central framework of Christian theology we have just recalled. Then the celestial and terrestrial world was seen as a hierarchy or chain of being which, viewed in ascending or descending order, embraced God, angels, man, animals, and inanimate nature. Whatever man may do, the physical or metaphysical universe is a divine harmony. In the first book of Hooker's *Ecclesiastical Polity*, in his survey of the reign of reason and law in the mind of God and in the world, he asks what would happen if nature should intermit her course, if the heavenly bodies should stop or wander, if the seasons should blend themselves in a disordered and confused mixture, the winds die, the rain cease, the fruits of the earth wither—'what would become of man himself, whom these things now do all serve?

See we not plainly that obedience of creatures unto the law of nature is the stay of the whole world?'

In the great chain of being, man occupies a middle position; he was made capable, as Pico della Mirandola said, of rising toward the angels or of sinking toward the beasts. He can do so because he is a self-governing creature. His reason is a divine gift; it can distinguish between good and evil and can, within limits, understand the purposes of a rational Deity. If man's reason, supported by his will, rules his appetites and passions, he is a godlike being; if his reason is not in control, his nature is a bestial chaos. By the fall, human reason lost much of its original brightness, so that man needs revelation and grace, yet he has a partly efficacious guide in his own right reason and in the collective wisdom based on the right reason of mankind. The whole doctrine of divine, cosmic, and human rationality and order is summed up or implied in the eloquent sentence with which Hooker ends his first book:

Of Law there can be no less acknowledged, than that her seat is the bosom of God, her voice the harmony of the world: all things in heaven and earth do her homage, the very least as feeling her care, and the greatest as not exempted from her power, both angels and men and creatures of what condition soever, though each in different sort and manner, yet all with uniform consent, admiring her as the mother of their peace and joy.

The emancipated modern intelligence may say that this picture is only the construction of a naive religiosity, is mere wishful thinking; but many notable minds over many centuries had helped to build it or shared it, and it was shared, in essentials, by most Elizabethans.

Among the fullest expositions in verse are the skilful didactic poems of the young lawyer John (later Sir John) Davies.

In *Orchestra* (1596), Davies took the dancing of men and women as an analogue or symbol of the measured harmony, established by creative Love, throughout the universe and all terrestrial life. (That symbolic idea, by the way, had been elaborately worked out in Sir Thomas Elyot's *Governor*, and a bit of Elyot's account is incorporated in T. S. Eliot's *Four Quartets*.) Davies' vision is not disturbed by the new astronomy, which receives no more than a parenthesis:

> Only the earth doth stand for ever still:
> Her rocks remove not, nor her mountains meet,
> (Although some wits enriched with learning's skill
> Say heaven stands firm, and that the earth doth fleet
> And swiftly turneth underneath their feet),
>   Yet though the earth is ever steadfast seen,
>   On her broad breast hath dancing ever been.

The other long poem, *Nosce Teipsum* (1599), was also in the Neoplatonic tradition, though Davies was drawing particularly upon recent French defenders of Christianity against Epicurean skepticism. The first part is on a text especially associated with Cornelius Agrippa's widely read book, the vanity and peril of man's desire for external, scientific knowledge, which caused the fall of Adam and Eve, as contrasted with his lack of the inward knowledge essential for life. Man is a paradoxical being set in a paradoxical situation:

> I know my soul hath power to know all things,
>   Yet is she blind and ignorant in all;
>   I know I am one of Nature's little kings,
>   Yet to the least and vilest things am thrall.
>
> I know my life's a pain and but a span,
>   I know my sense is mocked with every thing:
>   And to conclude, I know myself a man,
>   Which is a proud and yet a wretched thing.

These contradictions are not forgotten in Davies' more generally optimistic analysis of the nature of the soul and the grounds for faith in immortality. God made man akin to both angels and beasts, possessing a free soul which rules over his physical and mental faculties, though its directive light is darkened by 'the body's prison' and original sin. As a frail human creature, man needs grace and redemption; as an immortal spirit, he should welcome death as a second birth.

In Shakespeare the most familiar 'proof text' for the doctrine of order is Ulysses' speech in the third scene of *Troilus and Cressida,* which is in the humanistic tradition of Hooker and Sir Thomas Elyot. But the real evidence is in the plays at large, even though Shakespeare is so impersonal and undoctrinaire. We have only to put him beside some modern naturalistic writers to feel the total effect, to recognize that his characters speak, act, and are judged in relation to a religious and ethical philosophy of order, and are not merely observed with objective detachment or in a moral vacuum. One great and unmistakable illustration is *King Lear.* And if, passing by the question of final truth or falsity, we look at the Elizabethan ideology only as a writer's background, we must say that he could hardly have been better off. The traditional world-view offers an ideal and divine pattern or harmony both in man himself and in the world he inhabits, a pattern to which he aspires to conform; but because of his corrupt or lawless nature he is continually violating that harmony. In other words, the writer conditioned by such a creed had the fullest scope for feeling and delineating both the tragic and the comic aspects of the contrast between what man is and what man would be; he had a stage far broader and higher than that of the writer whose vision is limited to the actualities of human behavior in its immediate environment. Consider the scale and range of values in and between these familiar lines:

What piece of work is a man, how noble in reason, how infinite in faculties, in form and moving, how express and admirable in action, how like an angel in apprehension, how like a god: the beauty of the world; the paragon of animals; and yet to me, what is this quintessence of dust?

For a more religious statement of the same great paradox, we might take the opening sentences of Burton's *Anatomy*, which draw out the contrast between man as he was made, the most excellent and noble creature of the world, the principal and mighty work of God, marvel of marvels, the microcosm, the sovereign lord of the earth, created in God's own image, pure, divine, perfect, happy, and man as he has made himself, a castaway, a caitiff, one of the most miserable creatures of the world, so much obscured by his fall that, 'some few relics excepted,' he is inferior to a beast, living in strife and sorrow, subject to death and all kinds of infirmities and calamities, and to eternal misery in the life to come.

With this reminder of classical-Christian orthodoxy, we turn around to look, still more briefly, at the skeptical and naturalistic movement. In the Christian philosophy of man and the world and God, reason and faith supplemented and supported each other; skepticism led the natural reason to a more or less radical questioning of supernatural faith. Christian ethics added divine injunctions, a divine pattern, and the concepts of divine grace and salvation to the ethical ideals and imperatives arrived at by the ancient pagan philosophers; but, for such Christian humanists as Hooker and Milton as well as for Socrates, morality is natural to man because it is based on the universal absolutes of right reason. On the other hand, naturalism, both ancient and modern, set up man's in-

stinctive biological drives as natural in opposition to supposedly unnatural restraints. In much literature of the Renaissance, as in much of our time, naturalism had more to do with
sex than with general philosophy. And naturalism generally
went along with skepticism.

This rebellious mode of thought was only part of the larger
critical, anti-authoritarian movement which, like the philosophy of order, was nourished by the classical revival. The
critical spirit worked in many directions, from Christian
humanism itself, with its rejection of scholastic abstractions
for religious and moral practice, to political and historical
writing, the new realism of painting and sculpture, and of
course science, which profited from the whole intellectual climate and from the recovered works of ancient science. During
the sixteenth century, however, science proper seems to have
had a relatively minor part in fostering skepticism and naturalism, partly because it was only beginning and was not
widely understood, partly because, then as later, its effects
were not necessarily subversive. For example, the Elizabethan
Copernican, Thomas Digges, speaks of the earth as 'this little
dark star wherein we live,' and the modern reader may expect further remarks in the vein of Hardy's Tess, about its
being a blighted star; instead, far from being overwhelmed
by the thought of an infinite system, Digges is happy to think,
like many of his successors, that the greater the universe the
greater is the glory of God.

The main force behind skepticism and naturalism was the
rationalistic and rebellious intellect, which owed something
to science but was fed largely by ancient skepticism and naturalism and by such medieval doctrines as pantheistic Aver-
roism and scholastic Nominalism; the contribution of Nominalism was its division between reason and faith and its appeal to the particulars of experience against universal con-

cepts. And along with these modes of thought went the philosophic or unphilosophic pressure of 'libertine' individualism. For a few representative rebels of different kinds, there are such names as Machiavelli (for Englishmen the great embodiment of all kinds of Satanism), Pomponazzi, Étienne Dolet, Rabelais, Servetus, Montaigne, and Giordano Bruno.

As such names suggest, skepticism and naturalism had spread widely on the Continent. In sixteenth-century England, for various reasons, we find scarcely any evidence of heterodoxy except in denunciations from the orthodox. One example is an episode in Sir Philip Sidney's heroic poem in prose, the *Arcadia*. The young Pamela is urged by her wicked aunt to enjoy love freely in the April of her youth and to banish thoughts of religion, which is only the opiate of the people and has no meaning in a world governed by chance; to these largely classical arguments the girl replies with a passionate affirmation of Christian world-order and morality. Other Elizabethan writers took a similar line. About the only poets who can be called rebels are Marlowe and the young Donne. Donne we shall come to later, in another phase, and Marlowe is not quite a clear-cut case. It has been customary to identify him with his heroes and make him the great English spokesman of lawless individualism; but, if contemporary reports of his irreligious talk did not get in our way, we should probably think of *Doctor Faustus* as the most directly Christian of all Elizabethan tragedies. The drama can hardly be considered as a reaction to the new science, since Marlowe's astronomy is only a variant version of traditional theory, yet his scholar-magician is the very symbol of Renaissance intellectual *hybris,* and we might well take his aspirations and his doom as a main text here. However, the play is generally familiar, and for our purpose, the illustration of disturbed orthodoxy just on the eve of the new scientific developments, there is a better example in Spenser, the great representative of Christian humanism among Elizabethan poets.

With Spenser at hand (and Donne in the offing), we may recall two widespread beliefs of their times: first, that ever since the golden age the sublunary world, including man, had been undergoing change and decay; and, second, that the world would end with the end of its third era, the two thousand years of the Christian dispensation. It is needless to heap up reminders, many of them from the greatest writing we have, of these and associated ideas in Elizabethan and later literature, of the melancholy specter of devouring Time, of the conflicts between full-blooded attachment to life and the contemplation of death.

Spenser's most explicit recognition of science is in the proem to the fifth book of *The Faerie Queene,* published in 1596. He contrasts the golden age of order and virtue with modern disorder and iniquity, and cites the changes in the planetary system. Even the sun, the 'great glorious lampe of light,' has, since Ptolemy, declined 'Nigh thirtie minutes to the Southerne lake.' This—quite apart from a mistakenly large number of minutes—may not sound sinister, but we must remember another established belief, the Aristotelian and Christian tradition of the changelessness of the celestial order. That old belief had been strongly shaken, if not shattered, by the much-discussed appearance of a brilliant new star in 1572; even the heavens, it seemed, were subject to change.

Spenser's great contribution to the subject, and one of the great things in English poetry, was the fragment, *Two Cantos of Mutability,* published in 1609, ten years after his death. The two cantos are an example in miniature, if the word may be used of a poem so massive in effect, of many of the finest characteristics of Spenser's art, but that richly decorative art subserves the statement of the sober theme. Starting from the mythological war of the Gods and Titans, Spenser has an undefeated Titaness, Mutability, challenge the sovereignty of Jove and the other deities. It is she, not Jove, who rules the world. A trial of her claims is arranged before the supreme deity, Nature. Doubtless the poet's religious scruples made him shrink from bringing the Christian God upon his mythological stage, but that he should use Nature—with her sergeant Order—as a virtual equivalent is a significant reminder of the orthodox classical-Christian view, already observed in Hooker.

At the trial Mutability presents her case. The four elements, earth, water, air, and fire, are manifest examples of continual change. Animals are daily slaughtered, and men pass from youth to age, from wealth to poverty, from good to bad. Then Mutability brings forth as a visual lesson an emblematic pageant of the seasons, months, day and night, the hours, and lastly life and death. All things and creatures are the prey of time and change. Even the deities are too; witness Cynthia, the moon, the very symbol of inconstancy, and the erratic courses of other planets. So, Mutability concludes,

> within this wide great Universe
> Nothing doth firme and permanent appeare,
> But all things tost and turned by transverse.

After a meditative silence, Nature gives her verdict:

> I well consider all that ye have sayd,
> And find that all things stedfastnes doe hate
> And changed be: yet being rightly wayd
> They are not changed from their first estate;
> But by their change their being doe dilate:
> And turning to themselves at length againe,
> Doe worke their owne perfection so by fate:

> Then over them Change doth not rule and raigne;
> But they raigne over change, and doe their states maintaine.
>
> Cease therefore daughter further to aspire,
>   And thee content thus to be rul'd by me:
> For thy decay thou seekst by thy desire;
>   But time shall come that all shall changed bee,
>   And from thenceforth, none no more change shall see.
> So was the Titaness put downe and whist,
>   And Jove confirm'd in his imperiall see.
> Then was that whole assembly quite dismist,
> And Natur's selfe did vanish, whither no man wist.

The verdict is, in plain prose, that universal and unceasing change is a fact, but that it is not a blind, haphazard succession of accidents; it is the way in which things grow toward perfection in the great evolutionary process ordained by God. Spenser's optimistic compromise is not novel; it is much the same as that set forth eleven centuries earlier in Boethius' *Consolation of Philosophy*. But it is the two stanzas that follow, probably the last he wrote, which reveal the poet's profound inward conflict and give the poem a large part of its power, a new dimension. For, with all his earnest will to believe, his heart is not satisfied with this traditional optimism; the rule of Mutability in life is too painfully clear to be explained away. And while this admission is almost forced from him, he catches at the assurance thrown out by Nature and looks beyond this scene of trouble to pray for the changeless peace of eternity:

> When I bethinke me on that speech whyleare,
>   Of Mutability, and well it way:
> Me seemes, that though she all unworthy were
>   Of the Heav'ns Rule; yet very sooth to say,
>   In all things else she beares the greatest sway.

    Which makes me loath this state of life so tickle,
      And love of things so vaine to cast away;
      Whose flowring pride, so fading and so fickle,
Short Time shall soon cut down with his consuming sickle.

Then gin I thinke on that which Nature sayd,
      Of that same time when no more Change shall be,
      But stedfast rest of all things firmely stayd
      Upon the pillours of Eternity,
      That is contrayr to Mutabilitie:
      For, all that moveth, doth in Change delight:
      But thence-forth all shall rest eternally
      With Him that is the God of Sabbaoth hight:
O! that great Sabbaoth God, grant me that Sabaoths sight.

As in expounding an orthodox optimism Spenser was medieval, so here, where he is most deeply personal, he is medieval too. He is writing, or rather thinking aloud, in the tradition of *contemptus mundi*. He is facing the riddle of the painful earth, and his medieval instinct for unity and stability is upset; there is no answer to the riddle except in heaven.

We have taken account of some traditional reactions to traditional problems which have been only slightly or indirectly reinforced by scientific questionings. From now on, however, these problems will be largely conditioned by science. To return for a final moment to Shakespeare, we observed his indifference to science as such. Yet we may say that by 1600, the time of *Hamlet*, the finest of minds, grown restless and skeptical, is able to question traditional beliefs, to entertain the idea of life as meaningless flux, and to explore the depths of human corruption, and yet it has not lost its traditional ideal of inward and outward order and its faith in the actual or potential greatness and goodness of man. Modern writers have prided themselves on taking a good look at the worst; but no modern writer has looked farther into the worst than

Shakespeare, and he was able, though not easily, to surmount what he saw. It will be said, of course, that in modern times these questions have become infinitely more difficult because the ground that Shakespeare and his age stood upon has been undermined by science. That may be true; but it may not be a complete answer.

The New Science and the Seventeenth-Century Poets

We have surveyed the traditional classical-Christian conception of the world and man, the medieval heritage that was the
common possession of the Elizabethans. We shall now observe the impact upon that tradition of the new science and
the beginnings of the modern scientific and mechanistic view
of the world and man, a mode of thought partly prepared
for by Renaissance skepticism and naturalism.

In the seventeenth century there was much less disparity
between literary and scientific achievement than there had
been in the sixteenth. While literature maintained its Elizabethan vitality (with a heightened critical and philosophic
consciousness), in science this was, as Whitehead called it, the
century of genius, in Europe generally and in England particularly. To mention some distinguished names of only the
first two decades, there were William Gilbert, who propounded the Newtonian idea of the earth as a magnet and
argued for its daily rotation under magnetic force; Thomas
Harriot, the chief scientific mind in Ralegh's intellectual
circle, who made, though he did not announce, some of the
telescopic observations that Galileo was making; John Napier,
the inventor of logarithms; and Dr. Harvey. Other scientists,
especially at Gresham College in London, were busy, often in
collaboration with men of affairs, on the new problems that
were arising in various areas of technology. In these same

years Kepler's scientific imagination was evolving, from the
new data of astronomy, the laws of planetary motion; and
Galileo, along with his pioneer work in mechanics, was con-
firming the Copernican hypothesis by means of the telescope.
In *Sidereus Nuncius* (1610), Galileo reported his discovery of
the mountainous surface of the moon, the satellites of Jupiter,
and the innumerable stars of the Milky Way.

Some common misconceptions of the new astronomy and its
repercussions have been corrected in recent years by a number
of scholars. In the earlier seventeenth century the Ptolemaic
or Aristotelian system, though declining in prestige, was by
no means dead among educated laymen. It had the support
of tradition, of the Bible, of Aristotle, of the senses, and of
common sense, and it did after all explain the phenomena.
The Copernican theory, like Einstein's, could be properly as-
sessed only by mathematical scientists, and Galileo's demon-
strations were not known to or accepted by everybody. But
the conflict was not merely, or even mainly, between the
Ptolemaic and the Copernican systems. Kepler's master,
Tycho Brahe, the first great modern observer, had developed
a compromise that attracted a good many minds prepared to
give up Ptolemy but doubtful of Copernicus. According to
this theory, the earth remained the stationary center of the
orbits of the moon, sun, and sphere of fixed stars, while the
other five planets revolved around the sun. Thus there were
not two major theories but three, and all of them 'saved the
appearances,' though only the Copernican and Tychonic systems could be reconciled with the discoveries of Kepler and
Galileo.

As for the effects of the new astronomy upon conservative
thought and particularly religious faith, we are more likely
than not to exaggerate them. The mass of people had little

knowledge and less interest, and even the informed were not inevitably disturbed—as most of us have not been kept awake by Relativity. It has often been said that people who thought of themselves as living in a small, comfortable world were profoundly upset by the discovery that they belonged to an insignificant member of a huge system.* Well, a few men were troubled, as we shall see, but very few; and the idea just stated is in large measure a reading back into the past of modern feelings—feelings, moreover, which developed rather in agnostic than in religious minds. In the first place, seventeenth-century scientists, like the Elizabethan Thomas Digges, could happily accept an infinite universe as further proof of the Creator's glory. In the second place, people of earlier ages, even if not dazzled by our millions of light-years, had been fairly well accustomed to the idea of immensity. Had not the Psalmist contrasted the littleness of man with 'thy heavens, the work of thy fingers, the moon and the stars, which thou hast ordained'? And some classical writers, such as Lucretius and Ptolemy the astronomer, and medieval thinkers like Roger Bacon, were very conscious of vast space. Nor was the earth the supreme piece of God's handiwork; it was rather the basest part of creation, infinitely inferior to the changeless purity of the regions above the moon.

* To cite one recent comment, Professor Robert L. Schuyler remarks: 'To our ancestors, who lived with dignity and decorum on a stationary earth at the center of a tidy and well-regulated universe, with all the celestial bodies respectfully revolving around them in perfect circles, the situation in which we find ourselves would seem intolerably degraded' (*Proceedings of the American Philosophical Society*, 92 [1948], 47). The fact is that throughout the Middle Ages, from Ptolemy onward (not to mention earlier writers), the insignificant size and position of the earth were continually recognized. See, for example, the numerous witnesses mentioned by Francis R. Johnson, *Astronomical Thought in Renaissance England* (Johns Hopkins Press, 1937), pp. 36, 71, 108.

Finally, the Copernican hypothesis was only one of a number of problems, most of them of ancient origin, which revived with the revival of astronomy. We have noticed already the appearance of a new star in 1572 (and another appeared in 1604), which undermined the Christian and Aristotelian belief in the immutable stability of the heavens. There was the problem of the earth's daily rotation on its axis, an idea that gained acceptance in England earlier than on the Continent. And some speculations could be more disturbing than facts, such as the old notion of a plurality of worlds, of which the ill-fated Bruno was the best-known Renaissance exponent. If there are other inhabited worlds, asks Robert Burton, do creatures there have souls to be saved? We touched before, and shall meet again, the pessimistic and non-scientific belief in the decay of all nature, including man, as the world moved farther toward its dissolution. Many men who were apparently little affected by astronomical science could be disquieted by questions like these.

We took Spenser as a representative, just on the eve of the new science, of the conflict between belief in a divinely ordered world and belief in naturalistic flux. In *The Faerie Queene* as a whole, however, Spenser had been displaying examples of virtue and vice in action, as the serious modern novelist does (except that the modern novelist confines himself almost wholly to bad examples). This concentration upon practical ethics, which pushes cosmology into the background, was characteristic of the humanist tradition, and it is further exemplified in two contemporaries of Spenser who long outlived him, George Chapman and Fulke Greville. Montaigne had at great length demonstrated the futility of the human senses and reason, the impossibility of any real knowl-

edge, and such Pyrrhonist skepticism had led him on to naturalism, to the acceptance of custom and his own nature as
practical guides. Chapman and Greville were both tough-
minded realists, with no illusions about the prevalence of virtue in the world, but both were preachers of the ethical and
religious absolutes of Christian humanism. I mention them
here because both, with their vision focused on the nature
and behavior of man, give only passing glances to the new
astronomy. *The Tears of Peace* (1609) is Chapman's fullest
direct statement of the gospel of Christian Stoicism which he
expounded in his tragedies and even in his noble version of
Homer. He urges men to translate learning into active moral
wisdom, the rational control of the body's appetites and passions; that is 'the rich crown of old Humanity.' In the in-
duction to the poem the idea of a moving earth becomes a
symbol of moral disorder:

> Heaven moves so far off that men say it stands;
> And Earth is turned the true and moving Heaven;
> And so 'tis left; and so is all truth driven
> From her false bosom; all is left alone,
> Till all be ordered with confusion.

Fulke Greville has a vision similar to Chapman's of disorder in the soul and in society. In *A Treaty of Human Learning* he goes beyond Sir John Davies in an elaborate and vehement exposition of the deceitful uncertainty and confusion
of all human and secular knowledge. The cosmos of his poetry
is normally the old world of the spheres and the four elements, and he uses the new astronomy as one of the countless
examples of man's ignorance. We try to penetrate the secrets
of Nature, who makes 'The loadstone, sea, the souls of men,
and winds.'

Nay we do bring the influence of stars,
Yea God himself even under moulds of arts;
Yet all our arts cannot prevail so far
As to confirm our eyes, resolve our hearts,
    Whether the heavens do stand still or move,
    Were fram'd by chance, antipathy, or love?

But uncertainty about the celestial system is, as I said, only one of countless examples, and Greville finds the causes of man's fatal ignorance and misery within, not outside, himself. Though a prominent statesman and courtier, Greville never forgets that man is a fallen creature. As he surveys the world and all the arts and sciences, he sees in man everywhere not humility but irreligious pride, built 'Upon the false foundation of his guilt.' Having lost the true way, man seeks 'To govern God, and not be governed.' Such an attack upon man's intellectual pretensions and errors might seem to be the prelude to an obscurantist rejection of all learning. But Greville is also a Renaissance humanist, and he will not plead for ignorance as 'the mother of devotion.' He does urge that the arts and sciences, now such overgrown and confused bodies of abstract theory, must be purged of irrelevant intellectualism, given unity and stability, and made fruitful for use. Like Chapman, but with more religious emphasis, Greville insists upon learning as wisdom for the conduct of life; and that wisdom must be founded on nature and the one 'sure rock of truth, God's word, or pen.' True learning is

                    in the humble heart
        A spiritual work, raising God's image, rased
        By our transgression.

Spenser and Davies, Chapman and Greville, and other poets, such as Daniel, were conservatives who, with individual variations, upheld orthodox Christian humanism. Their younger contemporary, John Donne, was, through circumstance and temperament, a rebel. Nowadays everyone is an expert in Donne and there is no need for discussion of his early revolt against both ethical and poetical orthodoxy or of the course of his development. We may look first at the scientific allusions in his poetry, and these, though important, are less novel than they are sometimes made out to be. If readers were given a psychological test, the first response evoked by the phrase 'Donne and science' would probably be 'the figure of the compasses,' since one does not forget the simile of the rotating and the fixed leg of a compass applied to a man leaving his beloved wife for a journey. But the image was of the kind used in emblem books and was not itself Donne's invention; as scholars have pointed out, it was paralleled and perhaps suggested by a poem by the Italian pastoral writer Guarini. In the body of Donne's poetry a large proportion of the scientific images and language comes from alchemy (limbec, elixir, quintessence, electrum, concoction, tincture, dross, allay), from geocentric astronomy and astrology (the moving sun, concentric spheres and their 'intelligences,' music of the spheres, 'trepidation,' celestial influence on man), and from the lore of the bestiaries and emblem books (mandrake, cockatrice, phoenix, unicorn). In short, much of Donne's 'science' was the kind of thing used by the unlearned Shakespeare and others, and it was of course no less legitimate; Donne, like them, was not concerned with the scientific truth of such items, but with their value for the illustration of actual ideas and emotions.

For Donne's religious and philosophic reactions to the new cosmology we must turn to the prose and verse of his middle years, a period during which, for many reasons, he was in a state of worldly and mental insecurity and depression. In his treatise on suicide, *Biathanatos* (1608 or later), and his satire on the Jesuits, *Ignatius his Conclave* (1611), Donne showed his knowledge of Copernicus, Kepler, and Galileo's new *Sidereus Nuncius.* The two *Anniversaries,* published in 1611 and 1612, several years before he took orders, were nominally elegies on the young daughter of his patron but really meditations on the sinful corruption of man and the means of deliverance. The poems have some kinship with the *Cantos of Mutability,* though Donne's intricate tissue of argument is very far removed from Spenser's mythological and pictorial fable.

The young Elizabeth Drury becomes a symbol of the world's original divine beauty, order, and perfection, her death a symbol of its decay. One of the passages on the new science has been worn threadbare with quotation, but it must be quoted here:

> And new philosophy calls all in doubt:
> The element of fire is quite put out;
> The sun is lost, and th' earth, and no man's wit
> Can well direct him where to look for it.
> And freely men confess that this world's spent,
> When in the planets and the firmament
> They seek so many new; they see that this
> Is crumbled out again to his atomies.
> 'Tis all in pieces, all coherence gone,
> All just supply, and all relation.

These lines may sound as if Donne, whatever confusion the new philosophy has brought, were a thoroughgoing Copernican. He seems, though, like many other informed minds, to have accepted the Tychonic compromise; and in his poetry and the later sermons he often refers as a matter of course to a stationary earth and a moving sun. But what matters is his philosophical and religious attitude, not his precise astronomical views. We might suppose that an eager student of Kepler and Galileo would welcome new facts and theories without misgiving, but with all his curiosity and knowledge Donne is no scientific modernist. Like Spenser, he is instinctively attached to the medieval religious conception of a fixed world-order with its interrelated parts, and that great structure seems to be disintegrating. At this stage in the evolution of thought the idea of inflexible and self-sustaining natural law, which later was to become almost the definition of science, has not yet clearly emerged and established itself in men's minds, and new discoveries and old and new speculations may have a destructive and bewildering effect. It is not surprising that in the *First Anniversary* we find a mixture of new science, old science, and fable—Gilbertian magnetism, the appearance of new stars, the possibility of other worlds, the decline in the position of the sun, along with 'this world's general sickness' and heaven's apparent withdrawal from its old, intimate, beneficent relations with earth. The only help for man is 'The supernatural food, religion.'

In the *Second Anniversary*, which deals with the way of salvation as well as with the divine perfection that man has lost, there are affinities with both Spenser and Greville. Spenser put forth a theory of evolutionary perfectibility, only to give way to an overwhelming sense of actual mutability on earth and a prayer for the peace of heaven. Donne, for all his passionate hold upon life, turns, in the spirit of medieval *contemptus mundi,* from this scene of chaos, corruption, and illusion to contemplate death and the revelation of pure truth in the next world. After dwelling on scientists' disputatious ignorance of the human body and other things, he pictures the soul, freed from its prison of flesh, attaining at once the knowledge obscured on earth by the bodily senses:

> Why grass is green, or why our blood is red
> Are mysteries which none have reach'd unto.
> In this low form, poor soul, what wilt thou do?
> When wilt thou shake off this pedantery
> Of being taught by sense and fantasy?
> Thou look'st through spectacles; small things seem great
> Below; but up unto the watch-tower get,
> And see all things despoil'd of fallacies.
> Thou shalt not peep through lattices of eyes,
> Nor hear through labyrinths of ears, nor learn
> By circuit or collections to discern.
> In heaven thou straight know'st all concerning it,
> And what concerns it not, shalt straight forget.

This religious solution did not wholly satisfy Donne's mind, and in sermons the preacher could still be disturbed by the uncertainties of human knowledge, though these became argu- ments for clinging all the more closely to the Cross. At any rate, in such anti-scientific lines as those quoted, Donne's position is that of many thoughtful men of his time. He is declaring the fallibility of the senses and natural knowledge, and condemning the vain curiosity and pride which, while seeking to transcend human limitations, remains ignorant of the true light.

The great modern vogue of Donne inspired a fashionable tendency to see him as a skeptic, although, so far as we are aware, he never at any time approached doubt of the Christian faith. And there has been a related tendency to assume that the whole Jacobean age was wrapped in a dark cloud of scien- tific pessimism. As I have said, most men were not affected by science at all, and of those who were, very few were troubled.* In addition to Donne, about the only important witnesses that could be readily named are Drummond of Hawthornden and Robert Burton. In Drummond's *Cypress Grove* (1623), an essay in the tradition of classical consolations on death, one unclassical passage shows a reaction parallel to Donne's and some obvious echoes of the *Anniversaries*. Drummond catalogues human uncertainties about flowers and grass, the elements, the position and movements of the heavenly bodies, the existence of other worlds, and concludes:

Thus sciences, by the diverse motions of this globe of the brain of man, are become opinions, nay, errors, and leave the imagination in a thousand labyrinths. What is all we know, compared with what we know not?

The issue of his whole argument is an ecstatic Neoplatonic vision of man's soul leaving the dead body of flesh and ignorance for the pure light and illumination of its heavenly home. It is the solution of the *Second Anniversary,* and there are echoes of Donne's Neoplatonic phrases.

As for Burton, the 'Digression of the Air' in the *Anatomy of Melancholy* is the fullest and liveliest survey the period affords of the many and confusing astronomical ideas that had been circulating in learned books. Yet Burton, with all his

---

* To add one item, cosmology could be invoked by Thomas Campion, the lyrist and medical doctor, in one of his variations on the timeless theme of mutability and transiency:

> Earth's but a point to the world, and a man
> Is but a point to the world's compared centure;
> Shall then the point of a point be so vain
> As to triumph in a silly point's adventure?
>   All is hazard that we have,
>   There is nothing biding. . .

'Centure,' by the way, means the center, the earth; 'silly' means poor, helpless.

knowledge of the welter of facts and theories, does not take them tragically. He is amused, like Milton's Deity later, by the efforts of scientists to 'save the appearances,' but for the truth he is content to await God's final revelation. The reason is that his theme is the soul of man; and what he does take tragically, as we observed before, is the religious contrast between man's glorious potentialities and his actual degradation and misery.

Most of the writers we have noticed, from Davies to Burton, show more or less distrust of scientific inquiry and may perhaps be dismissed as obscurantists. At moments their attitude might possibly deserve the label; normally, however, it represented, not active hostility to science, but a strong conviction of the priority of religious and moral insight over knowledge of the external world—and some modern minds would hesitate to call that obscurantism. To cite one more witness, George Herbert was wholly concerned with religion and had little to do with science, yet he was aware that 'the earth is but a point in respect of the heavens,' and he wrote in praise of Bacon. The view that we have been meeting, and shall meet again in Milton, Herbert summed up, in his own special way, in a stanza of *The Agony:*

> Philosophers have measur'd mountains,
> Fathom'd the depths of seas, of states, and kings,
> Walk'd with a staff to heav'n, and traced fountains:
> But there are two vast, spacious things,
> The which to measure it doth more behove:
> Yet few there are that sound them: Sin and Love.

While Chapman and Greville and others were asserting that man and society must be saved by religious and ethical wisdom and discipline, their contemporary Bacon was asserting the prime necessity of scientific research and the limitless possibilities of man's dominion over nature. Bacon was aware of pessimistic doubts of man's powers and capacity for progress, and partly for that reason he may have minimized the difficulties and magnified the efficacy of his program and method. Among the obstacles that he discussed were the antagonism of divines and statesmen, public apathy, and, within the field of learning itself, the scholastic and literary tradition of university education and the unscientific allurements of alchemy and astrology. Bacon's critical analysis was, up to a point, quite valid. Scholastic and humanistic education had to a large degree been indifferent or hostile to science, and it was assuredly time that man should turn much more effort both to the discovery of scientific truth and to the promotion of material benefits. It was necessary that someone should call in the new world of science to redress the balance of the old, and Bacon was the first great prophet of progress, the Moses, as Cowley was to say, who led mankind within sight of the promised land. His influence became potent in the era of Puritan ascendancy, and his dream of co-operative research, which had already been realized at Gresham College, found special response in the group of eminent scientists who, after the Restoration, were formally incorporated as the Royal Society. They and continental scientists and philosophers paid willing homage to the great champion of experimental science. If, after three centuries of confident scientific progress (centuries during which many thinkers and poets issued minority reports), we now have doubts not merely of the millennium but of survival, Bacon can hardly be blamed for not foreseeing such an outcome. In his calm belief,

Only let the human race recover that right over nature which belongs to it by divine bequest, and let power be given it; the exercise thereof will be governed by sound reason and true religion.

But though Bacon would have been shocked by the way in which his prophecy has been fulfilled, he did, without knowing it, contribute largely to the current of thought that was both to exalt power and to make science the sole judge of truth. He was, as Marx was glad to recognize, the founder of modern materialism. Bacon was sincerely religious, according to his limited light, but, as a scientific heir of medieval Nominalism, he made a sharp cleavage between religious and scientific knowledge. If the senses, if experiment, alone led to real knowledge, religion and final causes would inevitably fall into the category of the unreal. Bacon complained that Plato and Aristotle mixed theology and logic with science, and he praised Democritus and others for removing God and mind from the study of things. That is obviously a proper attitude for the laboratory, but it may lead to the total repudiation of metaphysical and religious thought. Modern scientific positivists would wholly endorse both the principle and its corollary. Most modern psychologists would endorse Bacon's empirical and behavioristic approach to ethics, which was a conscious reaction against the idealism of the humanistic tradition. And many scientists and psychologists, but no humanists or poets, would endorse Bacon's account of poetry. Serious Renaissance poets, like those we have noticed and many others from Sidney to Milton, thought of poetry as, next to religion, the highest kind of illumination, and of the poet as a teacher and priest. Bacon, while granting some small didactic value, looks down from a scientific altitude upon poetry in general as wishful thinking, as an escape from reality, 'whereas reason doth buckle and bow the mind unto the nature of things.' Several generations later Newton, when asked his opinion of poetry, replied: 'I'll tell you that of Barrow;—he said, that poetry was a kind of ingenious nonsense.'

Within a few decades Galileo, Descartes, and Hobbes virtually completed the process of establishing scientific and mathematical truth as the only reality. Descartes did allow for God and the thinking mind as well as for matter, but his influence was largely materialistic. Hobbes, of course, made mechanistic materialism into a tight coherent system. For him nothing exists, even within the mind, except bodies in motion. Whether or not Hobbes's religious professions were sincere, his philosophy rejected the Christian conception of the universe for a mechanism started by a remote First Cause and rejected also the Christian and classical conception of man as a free and responsible moral agent. The appearance of such doctrines marked, in England, the dividing line between the old and the modern world, even though very few shared them, and though their author was, alone or with Descartes, the object of prolonged and vehement attacks from multitudinous defenders of orthodoxy. Nor did the scientists follow him. Such notable members of the Royal Society as Boyle, Hooke, and Newton were religious men who saw science and religion as complementary revelations of divine and indivisible truth.

In the earlier part of the century, while Descartes and Hobbes were writing, mystical modes of thought could still flourish, whether in the occult alchemical brains of men like Robert Fludd and Thomas Vaughan or in the clearer and finer minds of Sir Thomas Browne and Henry Vaughan, Thomas's twin brother. Dr. Browne, a physician and ardent scientist, author of a big and partly Baconian critique of traditional errors, was also a devout Christian and Neoplatonist whose contemplation of God, nature, and man rested on the old ground of analogy and correspondence. For him there are not impossibilities enough in religion for an active faith, and he loves to lose himself in the mysteries of divine wisdom. As scientist, Browne can seek objective scientific truth; but he has no doubts or fears because, ultimately, nature is the art of God, and the visible world is but a picture of the invisible. In Henry Vaughan we have a similar paradox, if it is a paradox. Though Vaughan's medical career may have begun with the virtual ending of his poetic productivity, we cannot imagine him disowning his earlier self, and he is the chief exemplar in English poetry of Christian and Neoplatonic mysticism. For him as for Browne the visible world is a picture of the invisible, and the world of the Many, which he loves, leads to contemplation of the One. Flower and cloud and waterfall and the dawn, all are hieroglyphics of God and of man's true life. But Vaughan is not, any more than Browne, a sentimental pantheist, simply because he is an earnest Christian, deeply conscious of sin. Yet the sinful soul, imprisoned by flesh, in a corrupted world, can achieve moments of vision in which the unity and harmony of all creation are made manifest.

Browne and Vaughan are examples, in the age of Descartes and Hobbes, of the happy marriage of science and mystical religion. The mind of Cowley was a smaller and shallower pool which reflected, with no ripples of disturbance, the passage of new ideas across the familiar sky. In his unfinished epic on King David, Cowley introduced a Baconian college into ancient Judea (as Davenant had lately put one into the medieval world of *Gondibert*); and in the same poem he expounded the old notion of cosmic harmony and of the world as the projection of 'the eternal mind's poetic thought.' He celebrated Dr. Harvey as the scientist who

> sought for truth in truth's own book,
> The creatures, which by God himself was writ.

He celebrated Hobbes as the man who overthrew Aristotle, as the Columbus of the new philosophy. The image of Moses leading his people to the border of the promised land Cowley

applied not only to Bacon but to the role of reason in religion.
He glorified the members of the Royal Society as 'Gideon's
little band' of victorious champions of true knowledge, and
he likened the discovery of such knowledge to the appearance
of a new star in the 'celestial dance,' which is an addition to
heaven's beauty, not a cause for foolish alarm.

Cowley's easy reconciliation of old and new was typical of
many minds, and in the later seventeenth century we find ourselves for the first time in a distinctly modern climate. In the
world of the new philosophy, a mechanistic and deterministic
world inhabited by mechanistic and egoistic beings, there
was little room for imagination and intuition, for spiritual
struggle or mystical contemplation. Even if poets did not accept the new creed, they could not help breathing a different
air. Men who had lived through the civil war and the Puritan
regime suspected and feared anything that savored of 'enthusiasm,' in either religion or poetry. In the expositions of
some Restoration divines, religion, while not actually reduced
to natural theology, took on the cool rationality which was
long to remain the mark of moderate and well-bred Anglicanism. What poetry could flourish in such a climate was
likely to be little more than direct commentary on men and
manners. Cowley in verse and Hobbes in prose commended
Davenant's *Gondibert* (1650-51) for providing that, for banish-
ing the supernatural and fantastic from heroic narrative. As
one would expect, much Restoration verse, and much of the
best, was satire. But while scientific rationalism helped to
nourish the spirit of satire, we might remember also such
rationalistic attacks on experimental science, on the enthusi-
asms of the Royal Society, as Butler's *Elephant in the Moon*
(the elephant proved to be a mouse in the telescope) and Shad-
well's *The Virtuoso*.

The desire for strictly rational representations of life and nature was a matter of expression as well as of central poetic belief and sensibility. An impulse that Bacon had started was carried much further by Hobbes and Restoration scientists and divines, a very conscious concern with accurate language corresponding precisely to objective realities. Bishop Samuel Parker even wanted an Act of Parliament 'to abridge Preachers the use of fulsom and lushious Metaphors.' Such semantic zeal, however desirable for science, could not but dry up the lifeblood of poetry. The rationalism of science (combined with the rationalism of neoclassical literary theory) pretty well extinguished not only the old images from alchemy, astrology, and the bestiaries (which were perhaps no great loss), but the symbolic use of classical myth, the emblematic and religious conception of nature, the whole complex of physical and metaphysical analogies that had bound together man and his world and his Maker. Augustan verse was inevitably marked by qualities that some call prosaic and some clear-headed.

Since the growth of scientific rationalism largely eliminated the mythical and the occult from the sciences * and from man's general view of himself and the world, it might be said that this first stage of the Enlightenment was a wholly salutary clearing out of the intellectual lumber-room—and, if we think of witchcraft, of the chamber of horrors. But we have observed or implied great losses as well as gains. In the scientific and skeptical air of the later seventeenth century both poetry and religion were in danger of suffocation—and no doubt some persons might regard that as the final proof of maturity. At any rate, religion and poetry by no means surrendered to the new materialism and determinism, to the

---

* The alchemical interests of Bacon, Boyle, Hooke, and Newton were not altogether unscientific, as the achievements of modern science have made clear (and as we noted before).

enthronement of scientific and mathematical truth as the sole reality. The fundamental issues, though now complicated by science, were much the same as those which, two thousand years earlier, had divided Protagoras from Socrates; and it was fitting that the modern Protagoras should have two of his most formidable opponents in the Cambridge Platonists, Henry More and Ralph Cudworth. In opposing Hobbes—and Descartes—these men could use scientific as well as metaphysical and ethical arguments, and their fusion of science with religion commended itself to such typically religious scientists as John Ray, the first great modern naturalist, and Newton. More's *Antidote against Atheism* was the starting-point for Ray's *The Wisdom of God Manifested in the Works of the Creation* (1691), and he frequently quoted More and Cudworth against those 'mechanic Theists,' Descartes and his followers. Though some elements in the philosophy of More and Cudworth were already or soon to be obsolete, some essentials were not, and were to reappear in later ages, including our own, to nourish minds that recoiled from mechanistic aridity. One can indicate their general position by saying that, while accepting much of the new science, they believed in certain metaphysical and ethical absolutes, in divine and human reason, in the reality of spirit and its primacy over matter, in man's freedom of moral choice, and, as we observed at the beginning of these lectures, in the unity of all truth, religious and scientific. In particular, they brought God back into the scientific universe through a reinterpretation of the Platonic *Anima Mundi*.

But our subject is poetry, and the great poetic exponent of Christian humanism was Milton—though we cannot take more than a short and bald survey of his attitudes toward science and of the implications of *Paradise Lost*.

As a young man at Cambridge, rebelling against scholastic studies, Milton had had a Baconian vision of a new era in the exploration of man's outer as well as inner world. Much later, in his tract on education, he gave practical science a far more important place in his curriculum than Renaissance humanists had been wont to do. He had not, however, abjured his basic belief that there is a gulf between the knowledge of external nature and the knowledge of God and the supreme ends of life.

When in the later sixteen-fifties Milton began the composition of *Paradise Lost,* Copernican astronomy had come into fairly general acceptance among the learned. So far as he utilized actual astronomy, Milton naturally followed the old pattern, which placed earth and man at the center of the world, but he indicated his knowledge of the other and made no explicit decision between them. The effect of the new astronomy was upon his imagination; it helped to give him a sense, at once easy and grand, of vast distances in an almost boundless universe. Since Milton, like the Cambridge Platonists (and like most contemporary scientists), had a firmly religious belief in the unity of all truth in a divine world, he was not appalled by the immensity of space. For the same reason, he could insist upon the essential oneness of matter and spirit.

But he could also, like the Cambridge Platonists, feel profound anxiety. While we do not know how far, handicapped by his blindness, Milton was aware of the growing strength of scientific materialism, at any rate his reaction was fundamentally similar to that of Henry More and Cudworth. *Paradise Lost* was the last great presentation of the traditional concept of one divine and natural order. For Milton, created nature is the old harmony and chain of being, and the recurring idea of the starry dance always kindles in his verse a half-mystical glow. His view of man is likewise the Miltonic version of Christian-humanist psychology: man possesses the divine gifts of right reason, Christian liberty, responsible freedom of moral choice and self-direction (though the author of *Paradise Lost* has less confidence in man than the author of *Areopagitica*). The theme of the epic is the violation of divine order in heaven and on earth, the contrast between irreligious pride and religious humility. And this theme is directly related to science, indeed to the whole problem of knowledge which is the great problem of the seventeenth century.

In the eighth book Adam, seeking information about the world in which he has been placed, raises the old question of cosmic economy—why the firmament should revolve for the benefit of the earth; and Raphael replies by outlining both geocentric and heliocentric systems and related ideas. But Milton's interest is not in the scientific facts, it is in the angel's warnings about astronomical speculation as an example of man's putting remote and secondary things before his primary end, the knowledge of God and the practice of the religious life. The episode is by no means a digression. Satan's revolt against the divine order is the supreme manifestation of secular pride. He brings about the fall of Eve by repeated appeals to the same motive; he misleads her shallow reason by extolling the glories of superhuman knowledge, which will make her a goddess. Eve, like Satan, represents what Fulke Greville had condemned as the desire 'To govern God, and not be governed.' How central this theme is in Milton's total conception is made still clearer by its emphatic reappearance at the very end of the poem. The humbled and illuminated Adam describes the Christian way of life, and the archangel Michael answers:

This having learnt, thou hast attain'd the sum
Of wisdom; hope no higher, though all the stars
Thou knew'st by name, and all the ethereal powers,
All secrets of the deep, all Nature's works,
Or works of God in heaven, air, earth, or sea. . .

And Michael goes on to speak of the pagan and Christian virtues, of which love is the soul; if Adam possesses these, he shall, though leaving paradise, possess a paradise within him, happier far.

The admirer of Galileo was not condemning science as such, and he was led by his own reason to theological and metaphysical heresies, yet some readers might say that his interpretation of the world and man was at best a noble anachronism, at the worst obscurantist Fundamentalism. Before we acquiesce in that verdict, however, we may glance at Milton's junior, the sophisticated John Dryden, the great representative of Restoration verse and an early member of the Royal Society. In the year after *Paradise Lost,* one of the speakers in Dryden's *Essay of Dramatic Poesy* showed the author's consciousness of scientific advance:

Is it not evident, in these last hundred years (when the study of philosophy has been the business of all the Virtuosi in Christendom), that almost a new Nature has been revealed to us?—that more errors of the school have been detected, more useful experiments in philosophy have been made, more noble secrets in optics, medicine, anatomy, astronomy, discovered, than in all those credulous and doting ages from Aristotle to us?—so true is it, that nothing spreads more fast than science, when rightly and generally cultivated.

Dryden was highly sensitive to currents of thought and literary fashion, and it is not surprising that he reflected Hobbesian ideas, metaphysical, ethical, and political. His heroic plays, with all their bombast about love and honor, displayed the working of such egoistic and naturalistic passions as Hobbes had described, and with hardly any appeal to reason or Stoic self-discipline such as Chapman had made. And when Dryden based an opera, *The State of Innocence,* on *Paradise Lost,* he carried one theme at least beyond the point where Milton stopped. That was the problem of free will and the related problem of evil. Milton's Adam, though in his first despair he had cried out against the situation in which he had been placed, came round to recognize his own responsibility. In Dryden's version, traditional doctrines are asserted by the angels, but a more stubborn Adam puts forth Hobbesian arguments for determinism and winds up with a protest against the hard conditions imposed upon frail man: God's foreknowledge 'Excuses him, and yet supports not me.'

But Dryden was less of a Hobbist than a skeptic, in the literal and philosophical sense of the word, and we must record the last stages in his quest of religious certitude. At the center of that problem was of course the relation of reason and faith. Dryden's plays had embodied a good deal of the traditional anti-rational Pyrrhonism that had been so notably expounded by Montaigne, and the skeptical denial of man's power to apprehend truth by reason might lead to atheistic nihilism or —as it led Montaigne—to acceptance of the established order. The latter solution was Dryden's. In the opening lines of *Religio Laici,* Dryden used the same image that Donne had long ago used in his *Biathanatos:* reason, like the moon and stars, is a dim light which fades before the sun of supernatural revelation. And in *The Hind and the Panther*—which appeared in the year of Newton's *Principia*—Dryden, putting behind him not only materialism and deism but even Anglicanism, found a final anchorage in the absolute authority of Rome. Although his elaborate religious arguments took little or no direct account of science, science had inevitably helped to nourish, in some men, a distrust of reason and a fideistic response to skepticism.

To refer, for a moment, to the opposite kind of reaction, there was Lord Rochester's vehement denial of the claims of man's reason to understand and govern himself or to pierce 'The flaming limits of the universe.' The skeptical libertine could only conclude with an angry acceptance of folly and knavery as man's universal condition and sensual pleasure as his only guide. Of Rochester's death-bed surrender to religion we need say nothing here.

Thus in the late seventeenth century we find the first real approach to something like the modern situation. Science is at the back, or the front, of most educated minds, and modern positivism has its great representative in Hobbes. While most men remain undisturbed, some are driven toward religious authority, some toward easy or bitter skepticism. Between these extremes there is a broad middle ground of more or less rational religion, occupied by many scientists, many good Anglicans, the Cambridge Platonists, and Milton. And if in common repute the author of *Paradise Lost,* in spite of his bold heresies, is accounted less 'modern' than Dryden and Rochester, a second thought might suggest that, at a time when science was just beginning its triumphal march, the old and disillusioned poet gave the one great prophetic picture of the modern waste land, that he anticipated what, after three centuries of science, has become a dominant note in the literature of our age. For the typical modern mind, however, the most significant of apples has been not Eve's, but Newton's.

III

Newtonianism, Rationalism, and Sentimentalism

George Saintsbury's phrase, 'the peace of the Augustans,' inflames the spleen of eighteenth-century scholars, who appear to have an especially sensitive regard for the credit of their sometimes abused period, and who would stoutly maintain that it was full of political, philosophical, and religious crises. Certainly we might hesitate to consider the age of the Duke of Marlborough, Jonathan Swift, and Bernard Mandeville as one of calm serenity. However, I am not an eighteenth-century scholar—as this discussion will doubtless make clear—and to an outsider the century, compared with the seventeenth or the nineteenth or the twentieth, does look relatively comfortable and relaxed. These same scholars, scenting disparagement as well as untruth in the conventional label, 'the age of reason,' appear to find more truth and more dignity in the newer label, 'the age of sentimentalism.' But, as a glance around our own world should remind us, quite contradictory labels can be true at the same time, and we may look at the eighteenth century through both lenses in turn—not that either one takes in the whole scene.

All ages are more or less conscious of disorder and all ages seek for order. The special characteristic of the early eighteenth century was a considerable assurance of having found it. We may take a brief survey of this well-ordered inner and

outer world under three headings: the theory of poetry, science, and philosophy and religion.

The theory of poetry was the coherent body of principles
that had been developed by Renaissance classicists and that
attained their fullest authority in England in the age of Dryden and Pope. Poetry is an imitation of nature, but—as critics
had begun to say even in antiquity—the best imitators of
nature had been the great Greek and Roman poets, so that
to imitate them is to imitate nature. If the English temperament resisted mechanical applications of the so-called 'rules'
of neoclassicism, it welcomed the fundamental principles. The
traditional didactic conception of poetry was sincerely held
and commonly followed. (One notorious example of didacticism, neoclassical personification, and science is the line Coleridge misquoted from a versifier of the latter part of the century: 'Inoculation, heavenly maid! descend!') The central
principle of decorum meant not conventional propriety, but
harmonious fitness of theme, matter, and manner. It meant
also that the material of poetry should be the universal
normalities of human nature and life, that it should yield
what Dr. Johnson termed 'just representations of general nature.' 'Poetry,' said Johnson, 'is the art of uniting pleasure
with truth, by calling imagination to the help of reason.'
Rightly understood, that definition was not prosaic or narrow
—though imagination, when called by a good many writers,
did not hear, and their reason or something was left to com-
pose frigid imitations of the ancients and embroider moral
commonplaces. At any rate such principles and practice implied a sense of ordered finality and, on the higher levels, a
sane and rational acceptance of both literary tradition and the
known facts of life and the world.

This attitude is reflected in the very structure and movement of the predominant verse form. Closed couplets, with

balanced or antithetical half-lines, made an ideal medium for objective satire or the exposition of established truth, but hardly for inward doubt, struggle, and vision. Also, in keeping with 'the grandeur of generality,' with the solidity of assured concepts, poetic language dealt largely in abstract terms descriptive of the typical rather than the particular. This tendency might seem incompatible with one that we noted earlier, the very conscious endeavor of seventeenth-century scientific thinkers to cultivate rational and precisely denotative language and get rid of the metaphorical and cloudy. However, eighteenth-century poetic diction was not merely a kind of pseudo-elegant inflation derived from Latin poetry. As Professor John Arthos has elaborately demonstrated, this diction grew to a large extent out of the effort of writers like Sylvester to naturalize in poetry the terms and concepts of science and philosophy; when the concepts died, the diction remained, but with its vitality gone. Further, though such diction preserved many petrified images, in general the carrying of a scientific ideal into poetry favored direct logical statement as against oblique suggestion and symbol. To the mind of Locke, metaphor and symbol are agreeable but not rational; if men would define their meanings and use words consistently, many of the philosophers' and poets' works might be contained in a nut-shell. For philosophic thinking, this is doubtless good semantics and good sense; it is ominous for poetry.

To turn to science, everyone knows Pope's epitaph:

> Nature, and Nature's Laws lay hid in Night.
> God said, *Let Newton be!* and All was *Light*.

Within a century William Blake assailed, as a great evil triumvirate, Bacon, Newton, and Locke. What lay behind Pope's exalted eulogy, and what lay behind Blake's vehement damnations? That, in brief, is the subject of this and the following chapter.

The idea stated in Pope's couplet refers especially to the *Principia* (1687), in which the movements of the earth and the heavenly bodies had been explained by laws of universal attraction. The image in which Pope clothed the statement reflected Newton's explanation of the prismatic character of light. Miss Marjorie Nicolson has shown to what an extent eighteenth-century verse was permeated with ideas and images of color and light derived from Newton's analysis, but although that analysis, as Miss Nicolson also shows, had its metaphysical implications, our two or three paragraphs must be concerned with Newtonian astronomy and cosmology.

On the scientific level, Newton's godlike achievement had been to bring the celestial system, with our earth, out of darkness into the light of order. Earlier scientists and philosophers had, to be sure, arrived at mechanistic descriptions of the cosmos (and of everything else, including the mind), but they had turned away from the medieval interest in final causes and the metaphysical question 'Why?' to ask the scientific question 'How?' The limited scientific answer had left the universe a materialistic mechanism of bodies moving in space and time; the secret of the mechanism was unexplained. Thus, though science had got rid of the providential regulation of God, its cosmos remained in some sense a chaos; hence it was possible for such a scientific thinker as Descartes to put forth his speculative theory of vortices. Newton, in demonstrating what William Gilbert had divined, the regular operation of cosmic magnetism, not only gave a scientific answer to the question 'How?' but gave at least a partial answer to the question 'Why?' A universe whose very regularity might have been called meaningless was re-established as a universal order under the sway of scientific law. But it is important to remember what was forgotten by a number of later eighteenth-century men (and has been forgotten by a number of modern writers), that Newton did not make gravitation an attribute of matter or the universe a self-running mechanism.

The consequences for metaphysics and religion are largely implicit in what has been just said. For most men in the eighteenth century, Newton was the great revealer of divine wisdom and power. The re-establishment of the physical world as a unified scientific order re-established the Deity on his throne, and not merely as a First Cause of motion. In religious belief Newton was, unlike the orthodox Boyle, an Arian or Unitarian, and his cosmology could become a natural prop of deism as well as of Christianity, but no one can miss the fervor or doubt the sincerity of the declaration of faith included in the second edition of the *Principia*. Newton sees everywhere in the universe the proofs not only of design, both majestic and minute, but of God's continuously active care. God is an eternal, infinite, omniscient spiritual being who is immanent in all creation and who is also, as we might not expect, the Father of man. We may remember that both Newton's scientific and his religious thought owed much to Henry More, not to mention more mystical writers.

For partial verification of these remarks, and for the typical reaction of a contemporary poet to Newton, we might pause over James Thomson's memorial poem of 1727. The poets, as we shall see, thought far more highly of Newton than Newton thought of poetry. Although parts of Thomson's poem are almost indistinguishable from his later eulogy of Pythagoras (in the third section of *Liberty*), still he does give a fairly specific account of the illumination provided by 'our philosophic sun.' Newton had explained tides and comets, sound and light. Suns and planets had rolled over man for ages, but Newton alone discerned and demonstrated causes and effects, and

by the blended power
Of gravitation and projection, saw
The whole in silent harmony revolve.

The heavens, which Descartes had misread, Newton

from the wide rule
Of whirling vortices and circling spheres
To their first great simplicity restored.

At his approach the stars

Blazed into suns, the living centre each
Of an harmonious system—all combined,
And ruled unerring by that single power
Which draws the stone projected to the ground.

Inevitably Newton's religious ardor swelled with his knowledge. He

from motion's simple laws
Could trace the secret hand of Providence,
Wide-working through this universal frame.

Could he who saw

The finished university of things
In all its order, magnitude, and parts
Forbear incessant to adore that Power
Who fills, sustains, and actuates the whole?

Formal philosophy has its great representative of scientific rationalism in Locke, the heir of Descartes and Hobbes and the philosophic father of such diverse children as Berkeley, Hume, and Hartley. I shall be very brief, because I share the feeling of a candidate I once helped to examine: when asked to discuss the sensationalism of Locke, she replied, 'I don't think Locke is sensational at all.'

Locke was given to quoting his friend, 'the incomparable Mr. Newton,' and the temper of a scientific age is everywhere apparent in his mode of analyzing ideas and mental processes, his insistence upon exact terms and definitions, his submission of all theories and things to the scrutiny of reason. From such scrutiny he does exempt divine revelation of matters of faith, which is superior to reason, though reason must judge if it be divine. Locke's rejection of innate ideas involved the denial of direct knowledge of God, though certain proof of an eternal source of all being is given by the knowledge of our own existence and the wisdom manifested in the creation. It is not impossible or unreasonable, since the great chain of being has no gaps below us, that there should be ascending species of creatures above us, more numerous even than those below. In ethics, Locke's rationalism is rather behind than ahead of that of Milton and the Cambridge Platonists, since he cannot very well share the great conception of right reason and sees the unquestionable principles of morality as revealed by the divine will in the Bible. At the same time the scientific philosopher can hold that moral law is as capable of demonstration as mathematics. (A couple of decades earlier, by the way, Thomas Sprat, the clerical historian of the Royal Society, had anticipated that science would be able to explain the soul through study of the body.) The modern mind, while perhaps impatient with Locke's half-measures, is of course on the side of his critical reason; and the philosopher's influence worked mainly in the skeptical direction. But if we think of the great souls of the seventeenth and earlier centuries—many of whom, in the eyes of Locke and his fellows, were tainted with 'enthusiasm'—we may ask if his systematic reason did embrace and illuminate everything. At least we might say that the spirit of Locke was about as favorable to poetry as that of John Dewey.

For our purpose, the heading 'religion' may almost be narrowed to deism, though that was an omnibus term for any unorthodox beliefs; and even defenses of Christianity against deism had a cool deistic air. However, in emphasizing the predominant rationalism, deistic or Anglican, we should not forget that the eighteenth century was the age of William Law and John Wesley, and that it was the great age of hymn-writing. We should not forget, either, that, if the upper classes were more or less pagan (so that Cowper could record the phenomenon of 'one who wears a coronet and prays'), and the lower classes enjoyed the pagan freedom of Gin Lane, a large body of the middle class retained enough of its Puritan heritage to welcome Methodism. But if we are thinking of men of letters and poets, we find much more of actual or virtual deism than of evangelicalism.

> When I survey the wondrous Cross
> On which the Prince of Glory died,
> My richest gain I count but loss,
> And pour contempt on all my pride—

that is decidedly less typical than Pope's *Universal Prayer*—which was often referred to as 'The Deist's Prayer'—or Addison's *Ode:*

> The spacious firmament on high,
> With all the blue ethereal sky,
> And spangled heavens, a shining frame,
> Their great Original proclaim:
> The unwearied sun, from day to day,
> Does his Creator's power display,
> And publishes to every land
> The work of an Almighty Hand.

The recognition of the universe as the work of an almighty hand has been a part of many philosophies and presumably all religions; it has been an integral though a secondary part of Christianity; and it constitutes a dominant strain in much deistic verse of the eighteenth century. But the deism which had its chief early exponent in Lord Herbert, brother of the poet-saint of Anglicanism, and which flourished just before and especially after 1700, was mainly preoccupied with the validity of revelation and the rational grounds of natural theology. This movement was the logical outcome of Renaissance skepticism, and it went beyond Locke in breaking—more or less discreetly—with Christianity. It was also an outcome of the Christian humanism of the Renaissance; it carried on the rationalism, without the faith, of Hooker and the Latitudinarians, the Cambridge Platonists and Milton. And such an eminently rational divine as Archbishop Tillotson—whom the deists were always quoting—might seem more calmly conscious of the wisdom of God in the creation than of sin and grace. Thus the growth of rationalism, skeptical or Christian, inevitably brought up the crucial question whether Christianity was reasonable; and what had been reasonable for the earlier rational Christians was no longer reasonable for the deists. We might have expected, in spite of the Boyle lecturers and other reconcilers of science and religion, that by this time aggressive deists would use scientific weapons; but in general they worked rather in the vein of what was later to be called higher criticism of the Bible, like their skeptical predecessors before the rise of science. (One influence on John Toland's pantheism, by the way, was Giordano Bruno.) At any rate this kind of deism could readily coalesce with Newtonian science and with deism in its broader meaning, with the conception, in Pope's words, of the 'Great First Cause'

> whose temple is all space,
> Whose altar earth, sea, skies.

Thus when we look at poetic theory, science, philosophy, and religion in the early eighteenth century, we find—whatever conflicts went on and whatever reservations may be made —a common and substantial basis, a belief in universal reason and uniform order. Moreover, since reason and order were seen not merely as remote ideals but as the operating principles of God, the universe, and man, such a creed could hardly fail to be optimistic; and it accepted actual evils as part of the divine scheme.

This brings us to another heading, sentimentalism, belief in a benevolent and beneficent universe inhabited by benevolent and beneficent man, a belief invincibly optimistic by definition. That at least is the popular strain of sentimentalism as it appears in a great mass of eighteenth-century poetry. The doctrine was in part a reaction against Hobbes's picture of a mechanistic universe and the egoistic passions of the natural man. It may also be said, like its immediate parent and ally, deism proper, to have grown in part out of traditional Christian humanism; one connecting link is Lord Shaftesbury's early interest in Whichcote, the Cambridge Platonist. To enlarge upon a comment made a minute ago, the hallmark of Christian humanism, up through Milton and the Cambridge Platonists, had been a faith in the rationality of God and the natural goodness of man and the dignity of his God-given reason—a faith that had often drawn from the evangelical the label 'Pelagian' or 'Socinian' or whatever the current term of abuse might be. But the optimism inherent in such a creed had had an ever-present check in a thoroughly religious consciousness of the reality of evil and of human weakness. As humanism grew less religious, optimistic faith in human virtue could develop unchecked. In the sentimental creed, summed up especially by Shaftesbury, the classical conflict between the rational soul and the irrational appetites and

passions, and the Christian war between spirit and flesh, tend
to dissolve into refinement of taste and spontaneous rightness
of feeling. Man's instincts, being naturally good, flow in one
direction. His moral sense generates a benevolent sympathy
between him and his fellow creatures and between him and
the universe. Such a creed was in obvious harmony with Newtonian science and the landscape, and with the abstract Deity
of deism and the deistic emphasis on doing good. Indeed some
writers, orthodox and unorthodox, used the idea of gravitation to describe ethical and divine impulses.

Before we turn to the poets, however, we should register
the fact that the earlier eighteenth century was not all sentimental sweetness and light. There were, for instance, divines
who thought religion was rather betrayed than buttressed by
appeals to reason and science. Then, in addition to the caustic
Mandeville, there were such great opponents of easy optimism
as Swift, Bishop Butler, author of the once famous *Analogy of
Religion,* and, later, Dr. Johnson. These three men, in their
several ways, carried on the rational, ethical, and religious
creed of traditional Christian humanism. Swift's account of
both the extravagant pretensions of science and the loath-
some Yahoos grew out of his primary concern with the nature
of man, his positive faith in the potentialities of reason, and
his religious consciousness of evil. Butler, whatever his philosophic inadequacies, took a broader, deeper, and more realistic
view of human nature and experience than either mere rationalists or sentimentalists. And everyone knows from Bos-
well of Johnson's massive common sense, his moral and religious earnestness, and his profound melancholy; much of
Johnson's best writing might be embraced under one title,
The Vanity of Human Wishes. Moreover, for all his interest
in scientific experiment, he insisted, in *Rasselas* and in his life
of Milton, that virtue and religion must precede the study of

physical nature; in reproving Milton for giving science so large a place in education, Johnson apparently forgot for the moment a main theme of *Paradise Lost.*

As we survey some poets, including a Christian or two, we shall meet, in various permutations, the various strains of thought and feeling that have been so roughly described. Pope, for example, Joseph Warton justly labeled the poet of reason; but that compendium of contemporary thought, *An Essay on Man* (1733-4), is in a considerable degree a versification of Shaftesburian ideas, partly filtered through Bolingbroke—and Pope's brilliant clarity exposes some central inconsistencies of the creed.

Although Pope satirized members of the Royal Society in the *Essay* as well as in the *Dunciad,* he had a consciousness of science, of a vast universe of worlds and other suns, of plastic nature and the magnetic dance of atoms, of global phenomena that science has measured and of creatures the microscope cannot discern. And the fact of scientific law has its share in the mechanistic doctrine that he half-unwittingly expounds. But, as in Shaftesbury's rhapsodic *Moralists,* the revelations of science, though they show man's 'time a moment, and a point his space,' are not a cause for dark dismay. Science, which may nourish man's pride, may also, with religion, nourish proper humility. It does not deny him his place in the stupendous whole or reduce him to an irrelevant accident; and it displays to the full the power and glory of the Creator.

Such attitudes we have met before, and Pope's picture of the best of possible worlds embodies many traditional ideas— the infinity of the divine wisdom whose beneficent purposes must remain hidden from the partial knowledge of man, the harmonious order of the great scheme of things, the

> Vast chain of Being! which from God began,
> Natures ethereal, human, angel, man,
> Beast, bird, fish, insect, what no eye can see,
> No glass can reach; from Infinite to thee,
> From thee to Nothing.

That vast chain of being, as we have seen at intervals, had for centuries formed a metaphysical, religious, and ethical pattern of belief; it was the all-comprehending manifestation of divine order. But, at least as it is set forth in Pope's dazzling chain of epigrammatic couplets, the doctrine seems to lose most of its old dynamic religious force and to issue in either a rigorous mechanistic determinism or a neat algebraic formula of sentimental optimism:

> All Nature is but Art, unknown to thee;
> All Chance, Direction, which thou canst not see;
> All Discord, Harmony not understood;
> All partial Evil, Universal Good:
> And, spite of Pride, in erring Reason's spite,
> One truth is clear, WHATEVER IS, IS RIGHT.

This faith, it must be acknowledged, is of the essence of traditional Christianity, and it was held by most of Pope's poetic predecessors; the difference is in the way it was held. If we think of the *Cantos of Mutability,* of Donne's *Anniversaries,* of Chapman and Greville, of Ulysses' speech on degree (or of Shakespeare at large), of *Paradise Lost* and *Samson Agonistes,* Pope's vindication of order and God's ways to man appears strangely glib and facile. That is not, to be sure, a novel verdict, but it belongs to our story. Pope was much too clever to be a philosopher. And the impression of glibness is not greatly lessened by the notes of genuine conflict and questioning, the recognition of man's passions and rebellious pride, of his being a god or a beast,

> Created half to rise, and half to fall;
> Great lord of all things, yet a prey to all;
> Sole judge of truth, in endless error hurl'd:
> The glory, jest, and riddle of the world!

Such paradoxes, however deeply felt, are much less moving than the sober lines quoted before from Sir John Davies. In the *Essay* at large, evil seems almost as abstract as the Deity whom the poet does not presume to scan; and doubts and conflicts are resolved or evaded by such comfortable doctrines as the equating of self-love and social.

Thomson's *Seasons* (1726-30) first appeared before the *Essay on Man,* but was much enlarged later. It had a long popularity because it did express a real love of nature and rural life and because, even more than the *Essay,* and more simply, it expressed the sentiments of a multitude of worthy readers. Thomson's discursive mixture of description and reflection and his pseudo-Miltonic blank verse and style are far from the pointed arguments and volleying couplets of the *Essay,* and yet the two poets have much in common. Resemblance is logical enough, since both are followers of Shaftesbury and are, especially Thomson, aware of science.

We took note of Thomson's tribute to Newton, and we should expect, in his pictures of natural scenes and phenomena, to find some science mixed with first-hand observation and with borrowings from the *Georgics*. The rainbow, 're-fracted' from a cloud, deludes the wondering swain, but 'the sage-instructed eye' recognizes the Newtonian prism. Milton had rejoiced in the mysterious powers of 'the arch-chemic sun' and its 'magnetic beam' or 'attractive virtue,' and the mystical dance of the stars. Thomson does likewise, in his partly Miltonic and traditional way. But Newtonian dualism stands behind Thomson's sun, which by its 'secret, strong, attractive force' rolls the entire system along; without its quickening glance the planets would be 'brute unlovely mass, inert and dead.' For Thomson as for Milton the 'optic tube' reveals the mountains and caverns of the moon. But Thomson can share with Pope the later speculations—of Locke, Fontenelle, and others—on man's limited vision and the animalculae that evade 'even the microscopic eye':

> Full Nature swarms with life; one wondrous mass
> Of animals, or atoms organized. . .

The more man knows and appreciates the wonders and beauties of nature, the more, like Newton, he reveres the 'Source of Being,' the 'Universal Soul,' the master-hand that 'the great whole into perfection touched.' And Thomson insists, much more than Pope, that the Creator is no absentee-God who merely started the world running. God's 'unremitting energy' and beneficence pervade the complex scheme of things. He stirs each atom. He launched 'the unwieldy planets' along 'The illimitable void'; and, should he hide his face, the sun and stars would reel and chaos come again. God's mighty hand, ever busy—to quote the *Hymn on the Seasons* and *The Castle of Indolence*—wheels the silent spheres and works in the secret deep and on the face of the fruitful earth; he 'fills, surrounds, informs, and agitates the whole.'

The great whole is of course 'The mighty chain of beings, lessening down'—as Thomson here puts it in Locke's terms—

> From infinite perfection to the brink
> Of dreary nothing, desolate abyss!

In the *Essay on Man* that conception is relatively static; in Thomson it is linked with a vaguely evolutionary—and Newtonian—idea of progress which comprehends both this life and its higher continuation. The combined ideas should satisfy those who complain of apparent evils because they cannot fathom the ultimate ends of the whole. Man may be cruel, but

> who knows, how, raised to higher life,
> From stage to stage, the vital scale ascends?

The dark state of man's wayward life on earth,

> This infancy of being, cannot prove
> The final issue of the works of God,
> By boundless love and perfect wisdom formed,
> And ever rising with the rising mind.

Everywhere, to cite the *Hymn*, universal love smiles around,

> From seeming evil still educing good,
> And better thence again, and better still,
> In infinite progression.

Or, finally, one may quote *The Castle of Indolence*:

> Up from unfeeling mould
> To seraphs burning round the Almighty's throne,
> Life rising still on life in higher tone
> Perfection forms, and with perfection bliss.

In the mundane sphere, Thomson is a champion of knowledge and progress on all fronts, from the mechanic arts and trade (which 'the big warehouse built; Raised the strong crane') to moral philosophy, the humanitarian 'social sense,' and the growth of liberty—this last the theme of another long poem.

This belief in material and spiritual progress involves a traditional inconsistency which hardly exists for Pope, who, though he celebrates primitivistic virtues, counsels resignation rather than effort. It would be hard to reconcile Thomson's firm faith in progress with his constant praise of the simple innocence of the golden age, as it flourishes in the work and

play of the uncorrupted countryside, and his frequent re-
bukes of the vices of the rich and proud in cities. But knowledge leads to virtue and religion as well as to material im-
provements. Science is a sister of religion and poetry, not an
enemy. Natural science explores and reveals the works and
ways of God; poetry makes such revelations vivid and intel-
ligible to mankind at large. Thomson's eulogy of Bacon and
Boyle and Shaftesbury and Locke and Newton carries on into
a eulogy of Shakespeare and Milton and Spenser and Chaucer.
They are all moulders of life and man.

Like Pope (and many other people), Thomson has the problem of reconciling the universal harmony maintained by an
almighty Providence with the actual ills and disasters of the
world, though he does not seem to be embarrassed by contradictions. He dwells sympathetically on the sufferings of humanity and animal and bird. Beneficent, life-giving Nature is
a world of death for man, who is the victim of beasts of prey,
of storms and winter snows, of plague, famine, and earth-
quake. And man, once 'The lord and not the tyrant of the
world,' lost his primitive innocence and learned

> the savage arts of life,
> Death, rapine, carnage, surfeit, and disease.

All creatures prey on one another. Man destroys harmless
cattle for food, and hunts harmless beasts for pleasure. When
he shows a sense of the dilemma, Thomson's answer, as we
have observed, is the same as Pope's: what to man's limited
vision seems vain or evil is really part of the total good. But
for Pope the best of possible worlds is a dialectical necessity;
for Thomson it is a truth spontaneously felt.

The rather dim name of Edward Young the general reader
may associate with the 'graveyard school' of poets, with a 'pre-
romantic' plea for original genius over imitation, and perhaps

with such tags as 'Procrastination is the thief of time.' Young's
Night Thoughts (1742-5) was a long defense of Christian belief, especially its central tenet of immortality, against liber-
tines, deists, and atheists; its main arguments had been set
forth in prose by the many apologists of an age in which religion was being seriously challenged. Science comes in, as
usual, by way of natural religion, which should be the rational
ally of revelation. Much of Young's material was the kind of
common property we have met: the chain of being; the greatness and the littleness of man, 'Midway from nothing to the
Deity'; the proofs of order and design in human life and in
the movements of atoms and of 'floating worlds'; the minute-
ness of the earth among a thousand systems; man's full knowledge of the 'mighty plan' in the next life; and so on. Young
has a sense of space more astronomical than Miltonic; and he
uses the idea (which Akenside, who has it also, assigns to Huy-
gens), that the vast distance of some stars makes it doubtful if
their beams,

> set out with nature's birth,
> Are yet arriv'd at this so foreign world.

What is more remarkable, Young gives a picture of the evolution of the stars, from 'fluid dregs' through successive stages
to blazing light:

> Nature delights in progress; in advance
> From worse to better.

Young's muse is so scientific that he can apostrophize 'Ye
searching, ye Newtonian angels,' and see an analogy between
Christ's life on earth and second coming and the return of a
comet. But 'Devotion' is the 'daughter of astronomy,' 'The
course of nature is the art of God,' and the starry dance a
'Fair hieroglyphic of his peerless power.' And with all his

appeals to nature and science, Young, like poets of the seventeenth century, sees man as

> More fond to fix the place of heaven, or hell,
> Than studious this to shun, or that secure. . .

> Love finds admission, where proud science fails.
> Man's science is the culture of his heart;
> And not to lose his plummet in the depths
> Of nature, or the more profound of God.

Sometimes—if not in lines cited—Young approaches poetry in his grandiose and earnest vision, scientific and Christian, of the universe and man and death.

> Jove claim'd the verse old Homer sung,
> But God himself inspired Young,

to quote the youthful Edmund Burke's rapturous judgment. *Night Thoughts* remained popular, at least with religious readers, for a long time, and it may have helped to kindle the cosmic imagination of the boyish Tennyson.

In 1744, while *Night Thoughts* was coming out, the young physician, Mark Akenside, who had already written a deistic *Hymn to Science,* published *The Pleasures of Imagination.* The poem has two main points of interest for us. Akenside had the avowed purpose of reuniting beauty and truth, poetry and science, the imagination and the philosophic mind—realms and faculties he saw as having been divorced in the previous age and divided between Dryden and Locke. Further, within the philosophic domain, he sought to fuse Platonic idealism with Baconian empiricism. Thus Akenside was bound to build an eclectic philosophical structure. But his dominant ideas are in line with Shaftesbury and Addison, and much of what he says about nature and science is the sort of thing we have met in Thomson and Young. We shall therefore consider the other and more special point, the claim sometimes made for Akenside as a minor prophet of evolution. Most of us, if asked about that idea in the eighteenth century, might think first of Lord Monboddo, who was so convinced of man's relation to the apes that, according to Dr. Johnson, he was as jealous of his tail as a squirrel. Akenside did not go so far as that.

In the eighteenth century some old and new beliefs stood in the way of evolutionary doctrine. One was the biblical account of creation, which, though it had long been reinterpreted in various ways, had also been worked out very concretely by some famous seventeenth-century divines. The notion was firmly established—firmly enough to remain an article of popular faith well through the nineteenth century—that the creation took place in 4004 B.C., on 23 October (one of the rival reckonings put the creation of man in 3928 B.C., on a mid-September day at 9 A.M.). Then the belief in fixed species was strongly supported by the conception of the chain of being as a vast but rigidly static series of gradations. As Pope said,

> On superior pow'rs
> Were we to press, inferior might on ours:
> Or in the full creation leave a void,
> Where, one step broken, the great scale's destroy'd.

And science upheld religious theory. John Ray's successor in natural history, Linnaeus, founded modern biology with his great system of classification, a system based on the assumption of fixed species. And that assumption had other props which need not be mentioned.

In the second book of *The Pleasures of Imagination,* God is said to have created the world in his desire to spread universal good, and to have not been content with one creative act. I quote the passage from the first version of 1744:

. . . through every age,
Through every moment up the tract of time,
His parent hand, with ever new increase
Of happiness and virtue, has adorned
The vast harmonious frame: his parent hand,
From the mute shell-fish gasping on the shore
To men, to angels, to celestial minds
For ever leads the generations on
To higher scenes of being; while, supplied
From day to day with his enlivening breath,
Inferior orders in succession rise
To fill the void below. As flame ascends,
As bodies to their proper centre move,
As the poised ocean to the attracting moon
Obedient swells, and every headlong stream
Devolves its winding waters to the main;
So all things which have life aspire to God,—
The sun of being, boundless, unimpaired,
Centre of souls! Nor does the faithful voice
Of Nature cease to prompt their eager steps
Aright; nor is the care of Heaven withheld
From granting to the task proportioned aid;
That, in their stations, all may persevere
To climb the ascent of being, and approach
For ever nearer to the life divine.

Nothing here or in the context or in the notes (which can be copious) indicates that the writer was conscious of launching a novel idea, and it was not novel. Akenside's notions of continuity may well have come from Plato's *Timaeus*, Leibniz, Locke, and the 519th paper in the *Spectator*, where Addison discussed Locke. But, without discounting these logical sources, one may suggest that much of the substance and some words are Miltonic. In the fifth book of *Paradise Lost*, Raphael's discourse to Adam begins, at lunch, with an account of angelic digestion which may seem quaint, but it leads into one of Milton's bold ideas. The discourse proper begins, fittingly, with that pivotal conception, the chain of being, but Milton proceeds to reject the traditional division between matter and spirit. All creation consists of 'one first matter,' which is forever, unless depraved, moving upward toward God. It is a universe of becoming. And, though the process has 'bounds Proportioned to each kind,' it seems to allow for plants transcending planthood, and for material man, 'Improved by tract of time,' turning 'all to spirit,' like the angels. In Akenside, as in Milton, the main emphasis is on a general process of becoming, of all life aspiring to God. What seems to be Akenside's one clear singularity—and neither poet's idea is quite clear—is God's continuous creation of new species to fill the void left by those that have advanced, though the perpetual ascent of being appears to be Miltonically qualified by the words 'in their stations.' At any rate there are new species and they develop. And there, for the time, we may leave evolution, until we come to a much more advanced scientist and far worse poet, Erasmus Darwin. But Young, with his vague nebular hypothesis, and Akenside, with his vague biological ladder, are examples of what Professor Lovejoy labels 'the temporalizing of the chain of being,' the gradual shift from a static to a progressive conception.

We cannot call the roll of the eighteenth-century poets and versifiers who, in a more or less enthusiastic vein, dealt with nature and science; though if we could, we should find the main ideas and attitudes that we have been describing, whether in association with deistic sentiment or with Protestant piety. Reason and feeling, science and religion are all revelations of God.

When the vastness of the Newtonian universe is fully recognized, we might expect man's sense of his importance to shrink. But that shrinkage, as we have seen, had gone on for centuries, and it seldom carried irreligious implications. In the early seventeenth century George Herbert could write a poem about man as the center of creation, for whom the winds blow, the earth rests, and heaven moves: 'The stars have us to bed.' Fifty years later, though still in the pre-Newtonian era, Thomas Burnet, in his imaginative and eloquent *Sacred Theory of the Earth* (1681),* censured as an absurdity in reason and a heresy in religion the idea, 'so derogatory to the infinite power, wisdom and goodness of the First Cause,' that 'all nature, and this great universe, was made only for the sake of man, the meanest of all intelligent creatures that we know of,' and 'that this little planet, where we sojourn for a few days, is the only habitable part of the universe.' Ten or twelve years later John Ray the naturalist, and the exponent of God's wisdom in creation, denied that the stars were made only to twinkle to us, and Richard Bentley, another notable champion of orthodoxy, said in his eighth Boyle lecture that God made the stars for nobler purposes. Thus man's throne may be lowered a little, but it is still a throne in the eighteenth-century poets. Edward Young, for instance, is not overwhelmed by the world of worlds that he envisions; great as that is, greater still is man's capacious mind, which 'Can grasp creation with a single thought.'

Nor has Newtonian science made the universe a repellent mechanism. The poets see the divine beauty of nature as enhanced, not lessened, by scientific explanation of its apparent mysteries. Contemplating the rainbow, Thomson exclaims, 'How just, how beauteous the refractive law.' Akenside declares that the rainbow never appeared so pleasing as when

---

* *Telluris Theoria Sacra* (1681-9) was translated as *Theory of the Earth* (1684-90); *Sacred* was added to the title of the 4th edition (1719).

first 'the hand of Science' explained it; and the same 'access of joy' and 'pure delight' is the privilege of those

> whose favoured steps
> The lamp of Science through the jealous maze
> Of Nature guides.

In the Restoration period the devout Robert Boyle had admiringly described the physical universe as a clock. Still earlier, Cowley, in his epic on King David, had invented a Judean scientist who

> Great Nature's well-set clock in pieces took;
> On all the springs and smallest wheels did look
> Of life and motion.

But Cowley was saying much the same thing when, in the same work, he described the universe as 'God's poem,' 'the eternal mind's poetic thought.' And in the eighteenth century phrases of both kinds express reverent admiration. When Young speaks of the 'vast machine' and the 'exquisite machine,' he is paying to the 'Great artist' the tribute of both scientific and religious wonder. The traditional affinity between the human and the divine poet was the theme of Collins' fine *Ode on the Poetical Character*:

> The band, as fairy legends say,
> Was wove on that creating day,
> When He, who call'd with thought to birth
> Yon tented sky, this laughing earth,
> And dress'd with springs, and forests tall,
> And pour'd the main engirting all. . .

Without accepting A. E. Housman's opinion that there were only four good poets in the eighteenth century and that they were mad, we may proceed from Collins to Christopher Smart and Cowper (we shall reach Blake in time). In Smart's *Song to David* (1763), the psalmist does not, like Cowley's scientist, take the works of nature's clock to pieces. In this magnificent canticle sentimental enthusiasm—the phrase does not bear its modern sense—and Christian faith are fused in a sustained rapture of adoration for the manifold and mysterious beauties of God's world. There is nothing like its energy, splendor, and magic until we come to 'Tiger, tiger, burning bright.' I can quote only some scattered stanzas:

> He sung of God—the mighty source
> Of all things—the stupendous force
>   On which all strength depends;
> From whose right arm, beneath whose eyes,
> All period, pow'r, and enterprise
>   Commences, reigns, and ends.

> . . .

> The world—the clust'ring spheres he made,
> The glorious light, the soothing shade,
>   Dale, champaign, grove, and hill;
> The multitudinous abyss,
> Where secrecy remains in bliss,
>   And wisdom hides her skill.

> . . .

> The pillars of the Lord are seven,
> Which stand from earth to topmost heav'n;
>   His wisdom drew the plan;
> His Word accomplish'd the design,
> From brightest gem to deepest mine,
>   From Christ enthron'd to man.

> . . .

> Strong is the lion—like a coal
> His eyeball—like a bastion's mole
>   His chest against the foes:

Strong, the gier-eagle on his sail,
Strong against tide, th' enormous whale
  Emerges as he goes.

             .   .   .

Glorious the sun in mid career;
Glorious th' assembled fires appear;
  Glorious the comet's train;
Glorious the trumpet and alarm;
Glorious th' almighty stretch'd-out arm;
  Glorious th' enraptur'd main:

Glorious the northern lights a-stream;
Glorious the song, when God's the theme;
  Glorious the thunder's roar;
Glorious hosannah from the den;
Glorious the catholic amen;
  Glorious the martyr's gore:

Glorious—more glorious, is the crown
Of Him that brought salvation down
  By meekness, call'd thy Son;
Thou that stupendous truth believ'd,
And now the matchless deed's achiev'd,
  Determin'd, dar'd, and done.

The theme of this poem, if not its range and fire, might be
said to be carried on in the familiar opening of Cowper's
hymn:

God moves in a mysterious way,
  His wonders to perform;
He plants his footsteps in the sea,
  And rides upon the storm.

For all Cowper's delight in nature, we might not expect scientific allusions in the work of such a quiet and devout recluse,
but he does refer to a number of the commonplaces—the

names of Newton and Boyle and Locke (and the less common name of Leeuwenhoek), the 'prismatic hues' of light, the telescopic wonders of the sky and the invisible wonders of the atomic and the insect worlds. And the earnest evangelical illustrates the earthward pull upon the soul by the image of gravitation. In mentioning Brindley the engineer and in crying out against merchants who 'Build factories with blood,' he also provides a slight exception to the poets' relative neglect of the practical science which was bringing in the Industrial Revolution—although, to be sure, the bubbling and loud-hissing kettle, which for the young James Watt was said to have raised problems of steam, to Cowper meant only cheerful tea-time.

What might be our chief expectation about Cowper is fulfilled in the poem *Charity* and, at greater length, in the third and sixth books of *The Task*. He praises science united with religion, but he denounces the vain measurements and pretensions of unbaptized science and urges the prime necessity of religious wisdom and practice. Cowper especially controverts the idea of a remote First Cause and maintains, like earlier poets and like Newton himself, that matter is impelled 'To ceaseless service by a ceaseless force,' the ever-active hand of God. But many poets and not a few divines, whether as deists or as Christian apologists appealing to natural theology, had glorified a rather abstract Deity. For Cowper, ceaseless force, the 'soul in all things,' is the same as for Christopher Smart:

> One Spirit—His
> Who wore the platted thorns with bleeding brows—
> Rules universal nature.

And the golden age that Cowper celebrates is not the primitivistic paradise of a fabulous past or rural present, it is that time in the future when all men shall be followers of Christ.

This sketch of the eighteenth century must serve, without providing full evidence, to suggest some general conclusions. In the first place, the triangular harmony of science, religion, and poetry had, like most triangular situations, not proved permanent. Whereas the earlier scientists, thinkers, and poets had occupied a good deal of common ground, the further development of science, of anti-Christian rationalism and evangelical Christianity, and of poetry was dividing a community of relatively homogeneous culture into groups embracing diverse and opposed kinds of knowledge and belief. Although one can prove anything by juggling with names, it is a typical fact that Pope and Thomson were much nearer to each other, and to Newton and Shaftesbury, than Cowper and Blake were to each other or to Herschel and Godwin. Secondly, whatever the varying capacities of the poets, they commonly move on the level of description and reflection, that is, on the level of prose commentary. In spite of the tendencies inherent in 'enthusiasm,' Collins and Smart are about the only poets—Blake being postponed—whose imaginative power rises to myth-making and symbol. The century does, however, reveal a movement away from the abstractions of natural theology and neoclassicism toward the individual, direct, and emotional apprehension of mystery and divinity in nature. And that brings us to our next topic—how far the romantic poets were conscious of science and of the poet's predicament, and how far they went in re-unifying the worlds of nature and man.

IV

The Romantic Revolt against Rationalism

The romantic movement used to be explained as a rebellion against neoclassicism, or as a return to nature or to the Middle Ages, but these and kindred impulses, as all modern students recognize, were only symptoms of a deeper and a unified change of heart. The last phrase is not casual; romanticism was a revolt of the feeling heart and the senses and the imagination against mere reason and its abstract picture of the world and man. Perhaps, because it is handy, I may quote an old attempt of my own at compendious definition of English romanticism: *

. . . a change from a mechanical conception of the world to an enthusiastic religion of nature, from rational virtue to emotional sensibility, from Hobbesian egoism to humanitarian benevolence, from realism to optimism, from acceptance of things as they are to faith in progress, from contentment with urban civilization to sentimental primitivism, from traditional doctrines of literary imitation to conceptions of the naive and original, from poetic preoccupation with the normal, the true, and the actual to dreams of the strange, the beautiful, and the ideal.

But to list these brief and unqualified commonplaces is to remember that the movement had been growing ever since the

* *Mythology and the Romantic Tradition in English Poetry* (Harvard University Press, 1937), p. 43.

later seventeenth century, that what we call romanticism was
a culmination as well as a revolution.

We may expand some of these headings just a little and
remind ourselves of some ways in which the romantic theory
of poetry enlarged and deepened what seemed to be the narrow and shallow limits of neoclassical and scientific rationality. The romantic poets are supremely concerned with 'man,
the heart of man, and human life,' but, since man and life
and poetry have been warped and deadened by the unnatural
and artificial, they seek the primitive and unspoiled in nature
and myth. The poet feels compelled to make a fresh start, to
penetrate the depths of being, outside and within himself,
and to link these two worlds together. He turns eagerly from
generalized and accepted abstractions to the truth of concrete
and diverse particulars—not without some stimulus, perhaps,
from the minute observation taught by the naturalists and
scientists. Nature becomes a main source of aesthetic experience and the myth-making imagination, a main avenue to
ultimate reality. The rich stream of classical myth and symbol, which had flowed through Spenser and Shakespeare and
Milton, had been dried up, or rather driven underground, by
the scientific rationalism of the Augustan age, but it emerged,
in the benign air of romantic idealism, to inspire nostalgia in
Coleridge and more than nostalgia in Wordsworth. In the
fourth book of the *Excursion,* Wordsworth revitalized Greek
myth as the poetic product of the religious imagination living
in close communion with nature; and for Keats and Shelley,
as for many European poets, ancient myth nourished those
visions of the ideal, that striving toward infinity, which were
central impulses in romanticism.

Thus the objective rendering of the normal and general
gives way to individual introspection and self-expression, and
formal order and decorum are less prized than emotional in-

tensity. Poetry, as always, unites pleasure with truth, but it does so by revealing the beauty that is truth. It does not call imagination to the help of reason (at least in Johnson's sense), but conceives of imagination as above reason, or as reason in its highest form of intuition. And, since reason is superseded or transcended by the senses and imagination, the poetry of rational statement more or less gives way to the poetry of image, symbol, and suggestion. The poet is not merely a moralistic, rationalistic, or fanciful commentator on life and manners; he is an original genius, a creator, a pilgrim of eternity and infinity. The Augustan age, if in theory it endorsed the sublime, in practice stopped well short of it (or had different notions of sublimity); the romantic poetry of imagination was, one might say, committed to the sublime. (And, along with the exalting of the idealistic imagination, we may note the virtual disappearance of one element of earlier sensibility and technique, namely, astringent, ironic wit.)

The traditional didactic conception of poetry remains, though it is understood in a much less literal way than in the eighteenth century. As Shelley said, 'The great instrument of moral good is the imagination; and poetry administers to the effect by acting upon the cause.' But the poets of the Renaissance tradition, to whom the romantics looked back, had held a view of the world and man based more or less firmly on Christian faith; the romantics stood outside orthodox Christianity and built their several creeds on nature, philosophy, and their own experience and consciousness. For the Renaissance poets, poetry was a subordinate ally of religion; for the romantics, it takes the place of religion. At the same time they are uneasily aware both of the poet's immense responsibility and of an unspiritual world's indifference to poetry.

Such changes in theory and practice imply, not the neoclassical ideal of ordered and uniform finality, but a realization that the semblance of order had been partly illusion, that man is enveloped by mysteries, complexities, and contradictions which mere reason cannot penetrate or resolve.

> Our destiny, our being's heart and home,
> Is with infinitude, and only there.

And that brings us to one main impulse in romanticism, the conscious and subconscious revolt against the Newtonian universe and the spirit of science. The eighteenth century had carried over from the seventeenth a religious or humanistic distrust of the large claims and the external preoccupations of science, but most poets of the earlier eighteenth century had enthusiastically welcomed Newtonian science as a great support of religion. It had also been a great inspiration for poetry, sublime and beautiful both as the projection of a vast celestial order and as the revelation of terrestrial light and color. Yet Coleridge, after sharing such views, could rebel against 'the mechanical system of philosophy which has needlessly infected our theological opinions, and teaching us to consider the world in its relation to God, as of a building to its mason, leaves the idea of omnipresence a mere abstract notion in the state-room of our reason.'

Taking a long view, we might explain Coleridge's attitude in terms of the age-old antagonism between Platonic and Aristotelian traditions and temperaments. In the middle of the seventeenth century we have an exactly parallel utterance from Thomas Vaughan, the poet's brother: 'The Peripatetics look on God as they do on carpenters, who build with stone and timber, without any infusion of life. But the world—which is God's building—is full of spirit, quick and living.' In the eighteenth century Newtonianism had gone through, in a larger way, much the same kind of cycle as Cartesianism had in the seventeenth—with the important difference that the revolt against Descartes had come from clearer understanding of his significance, while the later revolt was really directed against a misinterpreted Newton. The Cartesian philosophy had at first been embraced by men like Henry More as a new Platonic idealism suited to a scientific age, but, when its real drift became apparent, they—and Newton—recoiled from mechanistic doctrines. Newton and his earlier followers conceived of a universe of matter and spirit, a universe kept in operation by an immanent and transcendent God; but in the course of the eighteenth century the Newtonian system was cut loose from the divine hand, lost its religious and metaphysical sublimity, and became a self-sufficient material mechanism. Blake, Coleridge, and Wordsworth, in rebelling against a mechanistic universe and upholding an animistic one, were much closer to Newton himself than they realized.

Then the Newtonian universe might seem to have a counterpart in the inner world of the mind, if we think of old notions of the God-given soul and reason of man and of such corrosive agents as Hobbes, Locke, Hume, Paine, Godwin, and Bentham. Paine, that hard-headed deist, declared, by the way, that science, the study of the works of God, was now 'the true theology'; in youth he had turned to it and repressed the talent he believed he had for poetry 'as leading too much into the field of imagination.' David Hartley for a time put a spell upon Coleridge and touched Wordsworth, but his sensational-ist-necessitarian-religious compromise could not remain satisfying. To quote the later Coleridge ('The Theory of Life') for another general summary, 'from the time of Kepler to that of Newton, and from Newton to Hartley, not only all things in external nature, but the subtlest mysteries of life and organization, and even of the intellect and moral being, were conjured within the magic circle of mathematical formulae.'

Thus the romantic poets felt an urgent compulsion to find unity and spirituality in a mechanized and disintegrated outer and inner world. The eighteenth century—to put things very roughly—had accepted diversity as a fact of nature, but the general faith in reason and scientific law and the concept of the chain of being tended to reduce diversity to rational and static uniformity. The romantics, during and after the eighteenth century, sought an enlarged and enriched comprehension of nature and man, a more complex and dynamic unity than mere reason could construct. Most of them, whether or not they were philosophically sophisticated, were instinctive idealists, and the very philosophical and religious Coleridge, a disciple of the Cambridge Platonists among others, reacted in an essentially Platonist way against the mechanistic rationalism which had come to represent the spirit of science.

The search for unity and spirituality brings us to Blake, the earliest of the rebels and the one Titan among them. Many readers stop with *Songs of Innocence* and *Songs of Experience,* but these are flowers that blossom, so to speak, from the sprawling, tangled vines of the prophetic books; they are lyrical footnotes to the revolutionary gospel. I may confess my own inability to respond to much of Blake's creed as well as his vatic manner, but I will try to point toward his place in our story.

For one thing, though Blake's vision may seem quite unearthly, he shows far more prophetic awareness of industrialism than any of his contemporaries, far more than the voluminous and grimly realistic Crabbe. One reference is known to everybody:

> And did those feet in ancient time
> Walk upon England's mountains green?

> And was the holy Lamb of God
> On England's pleasant pastures seen?
>
> And did the Countenance Divine
> Shine forth upon our clouded hills?
> And was Jerusalem builded here
> Among these dark Satanic mills?

That gives a single sudden stab. Less familiar are such pictures of industrial progress as this:

> . . . intricate wheels invented, wheel without wheel,
> To perplex youth in their outgoings & to bind to labours in Albion
> Of day & night the myriads of eternity: that they may grind
> And polish brass & iron hour after hour, laborious task,
> Kept ignorant of its use: that they might spend the days of wisdom
> In sorrowful drudgery to obtain a scanty pittance of bread. . .

To turn to another question, the first lines quoted give a vision of the Lamb of God of primitive pastoral purity; but, in Blake's more complex conception, he makes over Christ in his own image as the seer and naturalistic rebel, the incarnation not of humility but of expansive vitalism, the enemy of restraint and 'moral virtue.' If Blake could thus transform Christ, it is not surprising that he likewise made over Milton, and his complete perversion has had a prolonged and deplorable effect upon readers of *Paradise Lost:* 'The reason Milton wrote in fetters when he wrote of Angels & God, and at liberty when of Devils & Hell, is because he was a true Poet and of the Devil's party without knowing it.' In using the words 'true Poet' and 'Devil's party,' Blake is of course turning accepted ideas upside down: the Devil's party is the inspired party, those who rebel against traditional authority and restraint.

For Blake the supreme thing is freedom and unified wholeness of experience. Imagination and impulse are alive, creative, true, and right, and must be obeyed; the restraints of reason are negative and false. This must be the creed not only of the artist but of all human beings, who are all artists, though they have withered under the manifold tyranny of compulsions and negations, political, economic, religious, and moral. The poetic genius, being the true man, is the source of all poetry and religion. 'All deities reside in the human breast.' 'Energy is Eternal Delight.' 'The road of excess leads to the palace of wisdom.' 'Sooner murder an infant in its cradle than nurse unacted desires.' Such maxims, which sound very modern, are, to speak with historical baldness, the radical culmination of sentimental 'enthusiasm' and optimism, the faith in spontaneous feeling and the natural goodness of man.

Blake's Devil is Reason, whose high-priests are Newton and Locke, with Bacon sometimes thrown in. In one place he lists, as groups of contraries, 'Bacon & Newton & Locke, & Milton & Shakespear & Chaucer'; Thomson, we remember, had made them allies. As Blake abhorred the mechanization of man in factories, he abhorred the scientific rationalism that dared to explain, in mechanistic terms, the mysteries of life and the soul and the universe, that laid 'hard cold constrictive' hands upon the vital and holy energies of imagination and instinct. 'Art is the Tree of Life . . . Science is the Tree of Death.' We, or those of us who abhor modern positivism, can sympathize with Blake's passionate hostility, though perhaps we should note that he did not distinguish between Bacon and Newton and Locke and their eventual influence. If he had known more of Newton at least, he might possibly have recognized that the scientist had given the poets a new sense of light (not, to be sure, the light of Milton or Vaughan); and that he had shared, in his own way, the capacity

> To see a World in a Grain of Sand
> And a Heaven in a Wild Flower,
> Hold Infinity in the palm of your hand
> And Eternity in an Hour.

That kind of vision we associate with Vaughan and Sir Thomas Browne and their fellows (among them John Ray), and Blake owed a good deal to the non-mechanistic strains in seventeenth-century and earlier thought, though his imagination also absorbed much later and cruder material. Since we listened before to Christopher Smart, we may recall Blake's best-known lyric as a supreme example of the renascence of wonder, a supreme anathema upon a mechanistic conception of God and nature and man:

> Tiger, tiger, burning bright
> In the forests of the night,
> What immortal hand or eye
> Could frame thy fearful symmetry? . . .

From that we might turn to the obverse side of the picture and quote some representative and relatively lucid lines from *The Song of Los* (1795):

> Thus the terrible race of Los & Enitharmon gave
> Laws & Religions to the sons of Har, binding them more
> And more to Earth, closing and restraining,
> Till a Philosophy of Five Senses was complete.
> Urizen wept & gave it into the hands of Newton & Locke.

Without venturing inside the Blakeian maze to provide a commentary on these lines, we may say that Los is the male and creative principle, the artist; Enitharmon the female principle; Har perhaps the stunted poetic genius of man; and Urizen mechanistic and repressive reason. This and much more we learn better from the critics—when they agree—than from the poetry (and Blake has been fortunate in his learned and devout interpreters). But, to fly in the face of current orthodoxy, we may think that the passage quoted illustrates the dangers of a poet's inventing, with aid from many cloudy sources, a complex, totally unfamiliar, and often inconsistent private mythology. It would be very satisfactory to say, as Blake's critics appear to say, that he supplied, in a superlative degree, what the eighteenth century had lacked, a myth-making vision which united an increasingly fragmentary and contradictory outer and inner world into a dynamic whole. Being myself no doubt a son of Urizen, I can only report that to me Blake seems to have poured out, like an erupting volcano, the raw materials of such a myth, and that he seems, moreover, to be one of those daemonic and Dionysian geniuses who overrate the validity of their visions and are overrated by their devotees.

To come to another major prophet, Wordsworth did not objectify his revelation in any Blakeian myth; nor, though he called the story of his mental growth a 'heroic argument,' was it a *Paradise Lost*. But the process of his development had such significance for him that a large proportion of his writing was an attempt to describe it, an attempt that he began before he had achieved any considerable recognition as a poet. Even in our brief study we must take account of the oft-told story as it was set forth, in retrospective terms, in *Tintern Abbey* and *The Prelude*.

Wordsworth looked back on his evolution as having had three stages. The first boyish phase was the happy animal life of a colt. With adolescence came an intense passion for nature, a purely sensuous and aesthetic passion for cataract and rock, mountain and wood. It was inspired by objects themselves, but was invested with 'an auxiliar light' from his own mind. To every natural form, even stones, he 'gave a moral life,' and everything that he saw held an inward meaning. The sense of communion and oneness with universal being was born from and nourished by frequent moments of ecstatic sensory perception, but it came to embrace love of the plain country folk whose lives were bound up with nature and who derived therefrom a simple nobility of soul. The humanizing of Wordsworth's sensibility inaugurated the third stage in his evolution, though the final phase was still some way off.

To a young liberal the French Revolution came as a natural and welcome event. But when its subsequent course extinguished what had been a religion, Wordsworth turned for support to philosophy—in particular, perhaps, Godwin's *Political Justice*. Uplifted by the promises of cool, unemotional reason, his 'hope . . . grew proud once more.' But he soon found that the problems of society could not be solved by mere academic rationalism, and, weary and sick of abstract logic and analysis, he 'Yielded up moral questions in despair.' It was now, when his second hope and faith had failed, that Wordsworth was brought back by his sister, and by Coleridge, to a realization of his true self and his original roots, his old trust in the spiritual power of nature to heal and inspire.

It is in the light of this great disillusionment with rationalistic philosophy, and the re-established primacy of the feeling heart over the reasoning head, that we must read the anti-intellectual and anti-scientific outbursts in *A Poet's Epitaph* and elsewhere, and also what may otherwise seem wild assertions about the moral wisdom in impulses from the vernal wood. Reason,

that false secondary power
By which we multiply distinctions,

had betrayed her votary, but

Nature never did betray
The heart that loved her.

Obviously Wordsworth, like Blake, is an outgrowth of eight-eenth-century sentimentalism. To realize, however, the in-adequacy—at least the aesthetic inadequacy—of such a label, we might recall, say, the familiar lines that describe the third stage of his evolution, when, though he has lost his early in-tensity of sensory perception, he can hear the still, sad music of humanity and has

> 　　　　　　　　a sense sublime
> Of something far more deeply interfused,
> Whose dwelling is the light of setting suns,
> And the round ocean and the living air,
> And the blue sky, and in the mind of man:
> A motion and a spirit, that impels
> All thinking things, all objects of all thought,
> And rolls through all things.

The loss of sensuous rapture and the more than ample com-pensation of richer understanding of one's self and richer human sympathy are also the theme of the later *Intimations of Immortality*. As the child grows into manhood his eye is less responsive to the outward beauty of earth, and even the radiant inward memory of the soul's celestial home gradually fades, but it is not wholly lost. Enough of this inward light remains to nourish an abiding consciousness of the reality and unity of all life and of the significance, *sub specie aeternitatis*, of human joy and suffering:

> Our Souls have sight of that immortal sea
> 　　Which brought us hither,
> 　Can in a moment travel thither,
> And see the Children sport upon the shore,
> And hear the mighty waters rolling evermore.

This is not the sea or shore that Newton thought of when he saw himself as a little boy gathering pebbles and shells on the beach, whilst the great ocean of truth lay all undiscovered before him; and no doubt the modern mind turns with relief to the scientist's conception of knowledge after the poet's beautiful hocus-pocus. And, in the age of Freud, or any age, Wordsworth's exaltation of the six-year-old child as 'Mighty Prophet! Seer blest!' may well seem bathetic nonsense—though the poet may have had in mind the very different sort of child who, with his imagination killed by pedagogy, becomes 'A miracle of scientific lore.'

It might be said that Wordsworth's conception of nature differs from that of eighteenth-century enthusiasts chiefly in being more vague and visionary. But that is not all. If the earlier poets' sentimentalism did not approach Wordsworth's animism, neither did their humanitarian sympathies rise to his passionate reverence for 'The native grandeur of the human soul.' In Thomson, nature is linked with the First Cause and with science, and the poet delights in scientific explanations of phenomena; Wordsworth's thought or feeling is altogether non-scientific * and is not concerned with evidences of design or indeed with much except his own response to the idea of unity of Being. Thomson carried no load of metaphysical questionings; Wordsworth is profoundly conscious of 'the burthen of the mystery,'

* For one exception, there is the passage in the *Prelude* (vi. 115 ff.) in which Wordsworth records his interest, at Cambridge, in geometry and astronomy, his meditations on 'Nature's laws' and the order of the stellar systems, the profound pleasure and transcendent peace he felt in recognizing in these

> A type, for finite natures, of the one
> Supreme Existence, the surpassing life
> Which—to the boundaries of space and time,
> Of melancholy space and doleful time,
> Superior, and incapable of change,
> Nor touched by welterings of passion—is,
> And hath the name of, God.

> the heavy and the weary weight
> Of all this unintelligible world.

Thomson is always a man observing and enjoying nature; his communion with it does not pass into self-surrender. Nor could he associate human destiny with the meanest flower that blows. Thomson's sense of man's oneness with the great whole stops well short of Wordsworth's:

> No motion has she now, no force;
>   She neither hears nor sees;
> Rolled round in earth's diurnal course,
>   With rocks, and stones, and trees.

Thomson's view of nature, however rhapsodic, scarcely goes beyond the detached and rational; Wordsworth's partakes of the character of myth, subjective myth.

Thus while Wordsworth was in the tradition of eighteenth-century sentimentalism, he had some affinity with the metaphysical and mystical—and scientific—idealism of the seventeenth century. His spirit that rolls through all things is less like the deistic First Cause, or Godwinian 'Necessity,' than like the Neoplatonic *Anima Mundi* of Henry More and others. And though he apparently was not acquainted with Vaughan, who had dropped out of sight, we remember that Vaughan gave a sentient life to natural objects, and thought of the soul as coming from—and longing to return to—a Neoplatonic heaven. Vaughan, however, thinks of the child's innocence of sin, not of his supposed insight into the mysteries of life (which is very far from Plato); and neither Vaughan nor More could ever have conceived of nature as

> the nurse,
> The guide, the guardian of my heart, and soul
> Of all my moral being.

Vaughan and More, whatever they allowed to nature, held unquestioningly to Christian faith and had a Christian sense of evil. Wordsworth, having no such faith, and no religious sense of evil, could satisfy his soul only by making nature supernatural.

He himself, of course, came to distrust the moral guidance of nature and spontaneous feeling, even in the period when he was affirming it—as in the early *Resolution and Independence*. Later, in the *Ode to Duty,* Wordsworth explicitly, though not without nostalgia, subordinated spontaneity to Stoic self-control. The new law of reason, greatly strengthened by grief for the death of his brother, was set forth in *The Happy Warrior* and *Elegiac Stanzas Suggested by a Picture of Peele Castle.* There followed *Laodamia* and the long *Excursion,* with its constant appeals to the peace of mind won through both Stoic reason and Christian piety; and, finally, there were the Christian sentiments added to the *Prelude.* Wordsworth's progress from trust in feeling through Roman Stoicism to more or less orthodox Christianity and general conservatism is no doubt a record of poetical decline (though the poems mentioned and others are not to be sniffed at), but that old question lies outside our range.

To return to science, we must go back to Wordsworth's earlier years and quote the much-quoted passage from the preface to the second edition of *Lyrical Ballads* (1800):

Poetry is the first and last of all knowledge—it is as immortal as the heart of man. If the labours of men of science should ever create any material revolution, direct or indirect, in our condition, and in the impressions which we habitually receive, the poet will sleep then no more than at present; he will be ready to follow the steps of the man of science, not only in those general indirect effects, but he will be at his side, carrying sensation into the midst of the objects of the science itself. The remotest discoveries of the chemist, the botanist, or mineralogist, will be as proper objects of the poet's art as any upon which it can be employed, if the time should ever come when these things shall be familiar to us, and the relations under which they are contemplated by the followers of these respective sciences shall be manifestly and palpably material to us as enjoying and suffering beings. If the time should ever come when what is now called science, thus familiarised to men, shall be ready to put on, as it were, a form of flesh and blood, the poet will lend his divine spirit to aid the transfiguration, and will welcome the being thus produced, as a dear and genuine inmate of the household of man.

In the first place, even in claiming science for poetic use, Wordsworth implies a gulf which had not existed in the early eighteenth century. Then, although his words sound brave and reassuring, they were to prove no more accurate than prophecies generally do. Wordsworth's conception of nature, the basis of his faith and his poetry, was hardly compatible with biology and the struggle for existence. Moreover, he could not foresee what a multiplied menace even machinery and gadgets were to become—the change, to go no further, from the surrey with the fringe on top to the sound of horns and motors in the spring. Above all, he could not, at that relatively innocent stage of progress, foresee that science was to alter the whole tempo and quality of human life and thought and feeling, that it was to transform not only the face but the soul of civilization and even threaten its survival. In short, he dreamed of the humanizing of what was to grow more and more inhuman.

Wordsworth did see clearly, however, the spiritual brutalizing of masses of mankind, and the rapacious and soulless commercialism, that accompanied the Industrial Revolution, which was of course a revolution in applied science. In the same preface of 1800 he made some observations which are verified a hundredfold by the world of today:

For a multitude of causes, unknown to former times, are now acting with a combined force to blunt the discriminating powers of the mind, and, unfitting it for all voluntary exertion, to reduce it to a state of almost savage torpor. The most effective of these causes are the great national events which are daily taking place, and the increasing accumulation of men in cities, where the uniformity of their occupations produces a craving for extraordinary incident, which the rapid communication of intelligence hourly gratifies. To this tendency of life and manners the literature and theatrical exhibitions of the country have conformed themselves.

And, contemplating the spectacle of men in a Christian land who are devoted to getting and spending, with no eye or heart for the realities of nature and the spirit, Wordsworth breaks out:

> Great God! I'd rather be
> A Pagan suckled in a creed outworn;
> So might I, standing on this pleasant lea,
> Have glimpses that would make me less forlorn;
> Have sight of Proteus rising from the sea;
> Or hear old Triton blow his wreathèd horn.

The sonnet is one of the first and finest expressions of the modern poet's sense of alienation from an industrialized and Mammonized world, a theme that was to run all through the poetry of the nineteenth century and to become a dominant strain in that of the twentieth. Our world has extinguished the myth-making vision that once was fed by man's intimate association with nature. It is worth noting that Wordsworth takes from Spenser the pleasant lea and Proteus and Triton, as T. S. Eliot invokes Spenserian health and idealism in a parallel context.

Wordsworth's specific allusions to science appear mostly in his later poems that people do not read, and his attitude varies. In the fourth book of the *Excursion*, after celebrating the ancient Greeks' mythological religion of nature, he delivers a vehement attack upon arrogant and unimaginative scientists who rather dive than soar, whose prying analysis of nature and the soul breaks down all grandeur and destroys the sense of divine unity and mystery. (The passage includes, by the way, an apparent echo of Milton's warning against vain astronomical speculation.) In the eighth book of the same poem, however, Wordsworth can speak with Baconian exultation of the mastery won by the thinking mind of feeble-bodied man over the powers of the blind elements; and he hopes that the conquest of nature may lead to fuller recognition of the supreme claims of moral law. We may observe too that Malthus' ominous *Essay on the Principle of Population,* which had appeared in the year of *We Are Seven,* did not shake the poet's faith that, though all creatures must perish,

> Yet, by the Almighty's ever-during care,
> Her procreant vigils Nature keeps
> Amid the unfathomable deeps;
> And saves the peopled fields of earth
> From dread of emptiness or dearth.
> (*Vernal Ode,* 1817)

But the burden of Wordsworth's later scientific allusions is that science, while it advances truth and material welfare, cannot explain the ultimate mysteries. To catalogue his sentiments would, however, make a poetical anti-climax, and we may end with the famous lines, added to the *Prelude* after 1830, on the statue of Newton at Cambridge, lines which are a late flash of inspiration and a calm assertion that science, or some science, need not be feared:

> The marble index of a mind for ever
> Voyaging through strange seas of Thought, alone.*

We would not expect much science from the author, omniscient though he was, of the *Ancient Mariner, Kubla Khan,* and *Christabel,* and we should be quite right. But we may remember John Livingston Lowes' discovery that

> The hornéd Moon, with one bright star
> Within the nether tip,

came from the *Philosophical Transactions of the Royal Society,* and that the same source, with Priestley's *Opticks,* suggested the 'tracks of shining white' and 'flash of golden fire' made by the water-snakes. The magic came from Coleridge. Of science proper we find hardly anything, except in the early *Religious Musings,* which includes tributes to Benjamin

---

* Some of Wordsworth's references may be recorded in a note. Quite often, especially in sonnets of 1833 (the year in which Lyell completed his *Principles of Geology*), he sounds like a nineteenth-century Young or Cowper. He speaks of 'the scale Of natures' fixed by God (*Presentiments,* 1830). In a set of sonnets, *Cave of Staffa* (1833), we hear of 'the almighty hand' of 'the sovereign Architect,' and of the presumption that would assign 'Mechanic laws to agency divine.' In *At Sea off the Isle of Man* (1833), he feels wistful regret for the imaginative and poetical age in which nature was impelled, not 'by laws inanimate,' but by active and visible powers of will and passion—a faint echo of the great early sonnet cited above. He goes on in the next sonnet to ask if we should regret that science has torn the veil from old fables, and answers that man's reason must still face mysteries which only religious faith can overleap. The sonnet *Steamboats, Viaducts, and Railways* (1833) reconciles, in the capacious bosom of nature, man's mechanical arts with poetic feeling. *To the Moon* (1835) similarly accommodates 'the searching mind Of Science' to God's glory. *To the Planet Venus* (1838) is less confident:

> Man now presides
> In power, where once he trembled in his weakness;
> Science advances with gigantic strides;
> But are we aught enriched in love and meekness?

Franklin, Newton, Hartley, and Priestley. The writer does not now see these men as repellent mechanists:

> Adoring Newton his serener eye
> Raises to heaven.

Seven years later Newton is pronounced 'a mere materialist.'

In the same poem we find, mixed with many other things (among them Cudworth's 'plastic power'), the traditional theme of eighteenth-century sentimentalists: it is our sublime destiny to know ourselves 'Parts and proportions of one wondrous whole,' which is animated and ruled by 'one Mind, one omnipresent Mind.' Such 'adoration of the God in nature' is the religious and philosophic refrain of such poems as *The Eolian Harp, This Lime-Tree Bower My Prison, Frost at Midnight, Fears in Solitude,* and the *Hymn before Sunrise.* Even *The Destiny of Nations* has some lines, very gritty ones, on 'naked mass (If mass there be. . .),' inertia, atoms, and Monads. Coleridge sees all creation as

> Symbolical, one mighty alphabet
> For infant minds,

and all things 'Evolve the process of eternal good.'

We may be reminded of the much-debated 'moral' of the *Ancient Mariner,* of the sinner's regenerating love of God's creatures. The implications of that theme we cannot here consider, but we may recall what happened to Coleridge's faith in nature in the poignant poem *Dejection* (1802). This ode the unhappy poet and husband addressed to Sara Hutchinson when he had just heard the first stanzas of *Intimations of Immortality* and felt that he had lost his own 'shaping spirit of Imagination.' I quote the later version:

My genial spirits fail;
And what can these avail
To lift the smothering weight from off my breast?
It were a vain endeavour,
Though I should gaze for ever
On that green light that lingers in the west:
I may not hope from outward forms to win
The passion and the life, whose fountains are within.

O Lady! we receive but what we give,
And in our life alone does Nature live:
Ours is her wedding garment, ours her shroud!
And would we aught behold, of higher worth,
Than that inanimate cold world allowed
To the poor loveless ever-anxious crowd,
Ah! from the soul itself must issue forth
A light, a glory, a fair luminous cloud
Enveloping the Earth—
And from the soul itself must there be sent
A sweet and potent voice, of its own birth,
Of all sweet sounds the life and element!

Coleridge, in the grip of profound physical and mental depression, feels the contrast between himself and the happier Wordsworth, who receives back from nature, as if it were nature's gift, the light reflected from his own mind. The melancholy Coleridge has lost that inward creative faculty, and the wondrous whole of the Almighty Spirit seems a flat and joyless picture of colors and forms and substances. It was left to the Coleridge of prose to describe what the poet had seldom achieved, the unifying power of the religious imagination.

When we look back on the romantic age, the most germinal minds appear to have been Blake, Coleridge, and Wordsworth, though 'mad' Blake had no influence and Coleridge's influence was felt chiefly through Wordsworth's poetry and his own later prose. Of the second generation of poets, much the most important for our theme is Shelley, but we can only glance at him as well as at Byron and Keats.

Byron, though doubtless incapable of consecutive or consistent thought, was far more concerned than the casual reader might expect with science, especially astronomy and geology. In *Cain,* for instance, he used Cuvier's theory of successive cataclysms in nature. But specific items are less significant than the general inter-reactions of science and Byron's religious and metaphysical beliefs and questionings. He had much of the Old Testament and of Calvinism in his bones, and he had also viewed the moon and stars through Sir William Herschel's telescope; and science helped to nourish both the awe and the agnosticism of an *anima naturaliter Hebraica* (and in some degree *Catholica* too).

Why I came here, I know not. Where I shall go to, it is useless to inquire. In the midst of myriads of the living and the dead worlds—stars—systems—infinity—why should I be anxious about an atom?

Sometimes Byron enunciates a deistic or pantheistic creed like that of Pope's *Universal Prayer:*

My altars are the mountains and the ocean,
Earth—air—stars,—all that springs from the great Whole,
Who hath produced, and will receive the Soul.

Sometimes the restless, world-worn cynic rings the changes on the littleness of man and 'the nothingness of Life.' He can, in *Manfred* and *Cain,* glorify the human spirit's quest of knowledge, yet

knowledge is not happiness, and science
But an exchange of ignorance for that
Which is another kind of ignorance.

So man can assert himself only by enduring his destiny, by opposing his will to the infinite will. Whether as Prometheus or Manfred or Lucifer, Byron feels himself one of those

> Souls who dare look the Omnipotent tyrant in
> His everlasting face, and tell him that
> His evil is not good!

Manfred's deep despair, unlike that of Marlowe's Faustus, 'is Remorse without the fear of Hell.' Yet Byron's defiances of God and the universe and society are the uneasy or desperate efforts at self-justification of a sinner and an egoist who cannot altogether free himself from Calvinistic beliefs and fears.

The only one of the romantic poets who had a scientific training was Keats, but his poetic themes and creed rarely admitted the medical, and in fact most of the images that might be called scientific are astronomical. We do not need to discuss Keats's quite unscientific passion for the moon, which provides the main symbolism of *Endymion,* but we may recall a few familiar bits from other things. In his first great poem, the sonnet on Chapman's *Homer,* the discovery of a new world of the poetic imagination is likened to the experience of

> some watcher of the skies
> When a new planet swims into his ken.

Probably, as B. Ifor Evans pointed out, the picture of the astronomer at his telescope has behind it the concrete fact of Herschel's discovery of a new planet in 1781, which was described in John Bonnycastle's *Introduction to Astronomy,* a book that Keats had won as a school prize. Bonnycastle's discourse 'Of the Nature of the Tides' may have contributed to another famous sonnet, 'Bright star,' though common knowledge would have sufficed. In this poem the sestet, which gives direct utterance to Keats's longing for Fanny Brawne, is an unhappily soft descent from the majestic and half-irrelevant octave:

> Bright star, would I were stedfast as thou art—
>   Not in lone splendour hung aloft the night
> And watching, with eternal lids apart,
>   Like nature's patient, sleepless Eremite,
> The moving waters at their priestlike task
>   Of pure ablution round earth's human shores. . .

Like Milton, Keats can look down on the little earth from the height of space, and he can also humanize the 'material sublime' in a vision both cosmic and sacramental.

If these two images represent the harmonious fusion of astronomy and imagination, two other items are anti-scientific —though one of them is not very serious. At that notorious dinner at Benjamin Haydon's, Lamb and Keats agreed that Newton had destroyed all the poetry of the rainbow by reducing it to the prismatic colors; and the fuddled and frolicsome Lamb persuaded the company, which included Wordsworth, to drink 'Newton's health and confusion to mathematics.' More important is the passage in *Lamia* where, apropos of the sinister sage, Apollonius, Keats exclaims:

>   Do not all charms fly
> At the mere touch of cold philosophy?
> There was an awful rainbow once in heaven:
> We know her woof, her texture; she is given
> In the dull catalogue of common things.
> Philosophy will clip an Angel's wings,
> Conquer all mysteries by rule and line,
> Empty the haunted air, and gnomed mine. . .

The sentiment is not altogether worthy of Keats's normal wisdom (and reappears, more appropriately, in Poe), but it has a bearing on the much-discussed intention of the poem and on the young poet's painful consciousness of the conflicting claims of the senses, the reason, and the heart. All his more significant poems are in some way related to that central and many-sided conflict. On the one hand, he had a miraculous sensuous endowment which demanded expression; on the other, he wanted to be, like Shakespeare or Wordsworth, a poet of 'the agonies, the strife Of human hearts.' And, to complicate that sufficiently difficult problem, there were the claims of the philosophic reason, which sometimes seemed to promise authentic light; yet sensuous intuition seemed to promise more, seemed able to 'burst our mortal bars,' to 'tease us out of thought,' and banish 'the dull brain' that 'perplexes and retards.' Keats did not live long enough to reconcile the cleavages in himself (if indeed he could ever have done so), but his awareness of them is a signal proof of his maturity and modernity.

Shelley manifested an ardent, if amateurish, interest in science from the tender age at which, according to tradition, he set fire to the butler; at Eton he electrified his tutor, metaphorically and literally, while making a sulphurous attempt to conjure up the devil. And science appeared in his poetry from *Queen Mab* onward, though we can only touch on his greatest work, *Prometheus Unbound*. Professor Grabo, following out the hints of A. N. Whitehead, called Shelley 'A Newton among Poets' and made large claims for his expert knowledge and use of scientific ideas and images. One source, by the way, seems to have been Erasmus Darwin, though Shelley also knew, at first or second hand, other scientists of his own and earlier times. Whether or not *Prometheus Unbound* is fully charged with electricity, we may at least grant that parts of Shelley's allegedly ethereal web of dreams have yielded a scientific meaning. But the validity of particular scientific data and images has nothing to do with the validity of the poet's vision of life, and that, to a good many readers, remains dubious.

In the first three acts of the lyrical drama, the spirit of man achieves, through love, a victory over inward and outward evil and brings in a Godwinian millennium of freedom from the bondage of law, convention, and religion. Emancipated human nature will show itself in all its natural goodness. Exempt from awe and worship, and free from guilt and pain, man can now (to echo Blake) learn to adore his own humanity. The fourth act, a later addition, is a symphony of rejoicing, and here assuredly science becomes more than peripheral. The millennium is to be not only spiritual but material. Love rules man, and beneficent man rules the forces of nature; the lightning is his slave. Such a fusion of the supposedly Christ-like with the Baconian may remind us of the very different vision of an earlier and older revolutionary, who saw sinful man, bereft of material comfort, seeking humbly to win a happier inward paradise of righteousness. But Shelley himself supplies a comment on his scientific utopia when, speaking of the way in which scientific knowledge has circumscribed the imagination, the poetry of life, he says: 'Man, having enslaved the elements, remains himself a slave.'

Romantics were defined by T. E. Hulme as all who do not believe in the fall of man. The phrase is suggestive, though it applies no more to romantics than to hard-boiled rationalists of the past or present, and it applies only in part to the romantic poets. The poet who most clearly had a traditional sense of sin, even if he rebelled against it, was Byron. Coleridge was for a time imbued with romantic optimism, but he could say in 1816: 'I believe, and hold it as the fundamental article of Christianity, that I am a fallen creature'; and his religious thought had of course a deep influence on the Victorians. Keats, while a believer in progress, was no 'Godwin perfectibility Man,' and had a realistic understanding of the human mixture of good and evil. But Blake, the early Wordsworth, and Shelley (at least till near the end of his life) held too strong a faith in the goodness of the natural man and of nature to think of man as fallen. They may see him as grievously misled, but they can hope to restore him to his lost paradise, and that is another matter. For them, as some moderns would put it, man is redeemable in history. The old religious creed and the old chain of being are not there as reminders of man's kinship with the beasts and his inferiority to God and the angels. Romanticism does not in general nourish humility.

As for the beneficence of nature, we have heard a good deal about that, and, since the doctrine of evolution lies ahead of us, I should like to end with a bit of optimism from William Paley's *Natural Theology* (1802). Paley wrote in the tradition of such works as Bishop Wilkins' *Natural Religion* and John Ray's *Wisdom of God Manifested in the Works of the Creation*, and his book was one of the general preparatives for evolutionary thought. Its subtitle was 'Evidences of the Existence and Attributes of the Deity, Collected from the Appearances of Nature.' While the *Natural Theology* did not attain the canonical status of Paley's *Evidences of Christianity*, it was held in high esteem, and it won the special devotion of the young Charles Darwin, who knew it almost by heart. I am not going into Paley's argument from design, but I do want to quote one passage which shows Nature's holy plan in exuberant operation: *

Walking by the sea side, in a calm evening, upon a sandy shore, and with an ebbing tide, I have frequently remarked the appear-

---

* Professor Howard Mumford Jones reminded me of this agreeable picture.

ance of a dark cloud, or, rather, very thick mist, hanging over the edge of the water, to the height, perhaps, of half a yard, and of the breadth of two or three yards, stretching along the coast as far as the eye could reach, and always retiring with the water. When this cloud came to be examined, it proved to be nothing else than so much space, filled with young shrimps, in the act of bounding into the air from the shallow margin of the water, or from the wet sand. If any motion of a mute animal could express delight, it was this: if they had meant to make signs of their happiness, they could not have done it more intelligibly. Suppose then, what I have no doubt of, each individual of this number to be in a state of positive enjoyment, what a sum, collectively, of gratification and pleasure have we here before our view?

And I cannot resist another bit, from this same chapter on 'The Goodness of the Deity,' in which Paley tries to explain the endowment of so many creatures with dangerous means of self-defense. 'But it will be said,' he admits, 'that this provision, when it comes to the case of bites, deadly even to human bodies and to those of large quadrupeds, is greatly *overdone; that it might have fulfilled its use, and yet have been much less deleterious than it is.' In fairness to Paley, it must be said that he sees nature's fecundity checked by nature's cruelty. However, to return to the joyful shrimps, instead of commenting on that partial proof that 'It is a happy world after all,' I am inclined to fall back on three observations that are not connected with Paley. One is from William James, who says somewhere that if at the last day a single cockroach were suffering from unrequited love, the fact would nullify any absolute idealism. The second is from that other eminent Harvard philosopher, Robert Benchley, who, when asked on an examination to analyze a certain fishing treaty, is said to have begun: 'I propose to discuss this question from the point of view of the fish.'

The third is a more serious and properly historical testi-
mony, which might well have been a bitter reply to Paley:
that is, Keats's badly written but arresting picture of the
struggle for existence:

'twas a quiet eve,

The rocks were silent, the wide sea did weave
An untumultuous fringe of silver foam
Along the flat brown sand; I was at home
And should have been most happy,—but I saw
Too far into the sea, where every maw
The greater on the less feeds evermore.—
But I saw too distinct into the core
Of an eternal fierce destruction,
And so from happiness I far was gone.
Still am I sick of it, and tho', to-day,
I've gather'd young spring-leaves, and flowers gay
Of periwinkle and wild strawberry,
Still do I that most fierce destruction see,—
The Shark at savage prey,—the Hawk at pounce,—
The gentle Robin, like a Pard or Ounce,
Ravening a worm. . .

Yet this and some other grim utterances, from Keats and
other poets, are only discordant notes in the symphony of romantic idealism and optimism. The typical strain is sounded
when Wordsworth proclaims

How exquisitely the individual Mind
(And the progressive powers perhaps no less
Of the whole species) to the external World
Is fitted:—and how exquisitely, too—
Theme this but little heard of among men—
The external World is fitted to the Mind;
And the creation (by no lower name
Can it be called) which they with blended might
Accomplish.

The romantic faith in nature, man, imagination, myth, and beauty was a genuine rebirth of the human spirit which still has meaning for us. And there is a meaning for us in the romantic revolt against mechanistic rationalism. Mr. MacLeish's *Einstein,* for instance, is roughly parallel to lines that Wordsworth addressed to the Utilitarians:

> an iron age,
> Where Fact with heartless search explored
> Shall be Imagination's Lord,
> And sway with absolute control
> The god-like functions of the Soul.

Moreover, the romantic protest against the mechanistic abstractions of science was essentially right, although it was not until our own century, as Whitehead observed, that science itself realized the necessity of reorganizing its concepts. At the same time it might be said that the romantic religion of nature rose above scientific rationalism without altogether meeting its conclusions, and that it was to prove quite inadequate for the nineteenth century. As for man, the romantics' large faith in the 'spontaneous me,' though it brought new depths of insight, meant a somewhat undisciplined and erratic ideal. The conscious quest of beauty likewise, while it yielded incomparably rich rewards, was achieved in a considerable degree by the ignoring of the solid—and perhaps sordid— world of actuality. Yet this brief and bald reckoning of profit and loss hardly constitutes a fatal charge against the romantics, since in our own age, despite our frequent condescension to both romantics and Victorians, neither science nor poetry has attained a satisfying creed. We shall try to see how in the nineteenth and twentieth centuries the heritage of romantic optimism passed to the scientists, leaving poets to the contemplation of a great void.

V

Evolution and the Victorian Poets

When we come to the Victorians, we are fortunate in having one great work, *In Memoriam,* as an inevitable focal center, and, though we must pass by a great deal, we may give the very representative Tennyson a little less meager space than we usually have for individual poets. The germs of *In Memoriam* were all present in the young boy, in the heritage he shared as one of a religious and cultivated family, in his temperamental capacity both for moods of intense depression and for mystical experience, in his earnest idealism and his desire for scientific truth. As artist and as thinker, Tennyson was a direct heir of the romantics; and from the beginning to the end of his long career he probably knew more of science, and was more concerned about its implications, than any other poet of the century. His boyish reading included Buffon and Sir William Herschel as well as the classical and English poets. In that astonishing comedy he wrote at the age of fourteen, *The Devil and the Lady,* he could apostrophize Love as the 'vast link of the Creation' and also describe man as a poor worm in a universe of never-ending space. And in his last volume, seventy years later, he asked:

Will my tiny spark of being vanish wholly in your deeps and
heights?
Must my day be dark by reason, O ye Heavens, of your boundless
nights,

Rush of Suns, and roll of systems, and your fiery clash of
   meteorites?

The answer is 'No,' but the poet had often been driven close
to 'Yes.'

In mentioning the romantics and their influence, by the
way, we should remember that, with the exception of the
minstrel Scott and the earth-shaking Byron, the poets whom
we look back upon were not the great figures of their time.
Byron summed up both critical and popular opinion when he
said, apropos of Wordsworth and the others,

> Scott, Rogers, Campbell, Moore and Crabbe will try
> 'Gainst you the question with posterity.

As a young boy, in the remote Lincolnshire parsonage, Tennyson shared the universal shock of Byron's death. How early
he read most of the other romantic poets we cannot be sure;
at any rate they were a major interest of his literary set at
Cambridge. In the eighteen-twenties and later, it may be
added, the most popular new books of verse were the insipid
Albums and Annuals; the thin and facile effusions of Mrs.
Hemans and 'L. E. L.'; Keble's volume of mild hymns, *The
Christian Year;* Robert Pollok's *The Course of Time,* a sort
of evangelical *Night Thoughts,* a picture in ten books of
human sins and the terrors of Judgment, which reached its
78th thousand in 1868; and the somewhat similar works of
Robert Montgomery, which Macaulay so ruthlessly—and
vainly—tried to exterminate. That was the taste of a rising
poet's public, and the wonder is not that Tennyson sometimes
wrote on the same level, but that he so greatly transcended
and raised it.

Although academic prize poems are seldom important, we
must notice Tennyson's *Timbuctoo* (1829), his first statement

of a problem that had been felt by the romantics and was to weigh heavily upon him, that is, the role of poetry and the poet in the modern scientific and industrial world. We touched earlier upon the romantic poets' revival of myth, which was both an instinctive and a conscious effort to reunite nature and the poetic imagination in the face of an increasingly mechanized universe and 'unnatural' society. The name of Blake is enough to recall the motive of his destructive and creative energy. Coleridge had sighed for

> The fair humanities of old religion,
> The Power, the Beauty, and the Majesty

of the old divinities of nature, which nourished the language of the heart but 'live no longer in the faith of reason.' Wordsworth's conception of nature and myth inspired Keats. Shelley contrived to be ambivalent (I must use that precious word once), to be at the same time the most spontaneous of mythmakers and the most scientifically minded poet of the age. The conflict was clearly formulated by the critics. In his first lecture on poetry Hazlitt said, in words that Keats echoed in *Lamia*, that the wings of poetry are clipped by the progress of mechanical knowledge and the advances of civilization. Thomas Love Peacock, with his hatred of 'progress' and his nostalgia for the antique world, saw poetry as inevitably declining from the golden age to the brass present. Even Macaulay, who was to become the very apostle of progress, in his first *Edinburgh* essay, on Milton, accepted the decline of poetry as the unavoidable result of advancing civilization.

At a time when such ideas were being put forth by men of letters, in a country which was rapidly becoming the workshop of the world, the traditional high claims of poetry, so lately reasserted by the romantics, might well seem shaken.

In Tennyson's prize poem, the poet, standing above the strait
where Hercules had fixed his pillars, and musing on legends
that once had their being in the heart of man, is approached
by a celestial visitant. It is the spirit of imagination and
poetry, who enables poets to see and express the truth implicit in the great body of fable, to minister to man's hopes
and fears, to teach him to attain the unattainable. But the
spirit's speech and the poem end on a less inspiring note. The
progress of civilization and science will bring about the decay
of poetry:

> Oh city! oh latest throne! where I was raised
> To be a mystery of loveliness
> Unto all eyes, the time is well-nigh come
> When I must render up this glorious home
> To keen Discovery: soon yon brilliant towers
> Shall darken with the waving of her wand;
> Darken, and shrink and shiver into huts,
> Black specks amid a waste of dreary sand,
> Low-built, mud-wall'd, barbarian settlements,
> How chang'd from this fair city!

We cannot follow up this and the related question of the
poet's social responsibility or aesthetic detachment; it is
enough to mention such poems as *The Poet, The Poet's Mind,
The Hesperides, The Lady of Shalott, The Palace of Art, The
Lotos-Eaters,* and *Ulysses.* That Tennyson felt a real tug of
war is made clear by the persuasive beauty with which he
presented the drugged enchantments of irresponsibility. And
to that problem were added the oppressive burdens of science.
Much later, in an unexpected epilogue to *The Charge of the
Heavy Brigade at Balaclava,* Tennyson contrasted the situa-
ation of the modern poet with that of old Horace, who could
strike the stars with head sublime,

> But scarce could see, as now we see,
>   The man in Space and Time,
> So drew perchance a happier lot
>   Than ours, who rhyme to-day.
> The fires that arch this dusky dot—
>   Yon myriad-worlded way—
> The vast sun-clusters' gathered blaze,
>   World-isles in lonely skies,
> Whole heavens within themselves, amaze
>   Our brief humanities. . .

Since *In Memoriam* appeared in 1850, nine years before *The Origin of Species*, and since it was being composed from 1833 onward, we must take a glance at the growth of evolutionary doctrines. The general idea of development and the special idea of natural selection were familiar to various Greeks and Romans, such as Empedocles, Aristotle, and Lucretius, but we can notice only a few late links in the chain. In a broad sense, the modern doctrine was a logical extension to both the celestial and the biological worlds of the historical concept and method which had been preoccupied with the progress of civilization; and we observed in the eighteenth century some signs that the static chain of being was becoming a dynamic idea. We noticed also some of the long line of writers up through Paley who, in showing the Creator's wisdom, had assembled more and more evidence of creatures' adaptation to their environment. But whereas these writers had no doubt of a purposive universe, modern science tended more and more to present or imply an endless process of natural cause and effect. We remember the answer of Laplace when that eminent Christian and humorist, Napoleon, said the astronomer had left the Creator out of his system: 'I had no need of that hypothesis.' On the other hand, Cuvier and English scientists in general were more or less orthodox. The

clerical sociologist Malthus, by the way, drew a picture of
human life which, for all his piety, might well have awakened
doubts of a beneficent Providence, and which gave both Darwin and Wallace a main clue to the struggle for existence.

The claims of Darwin's grandfather upon us are more scientific than poetical. Erasmus Darwin's chief work was *Zoono-
mia* (1794-6), but we shall look at his two long poems, *The
Botanic Garden* (1789-91) and *The Temple of Nature* (1803).
Seeking 'to inlist Imagination under the banner of Science,'
and to raise the scientific level of poetry, Darwin thought to
make exposition attractive by using, as decorative and symbolic personifications, the figures of classical myth and—far removed from their forebears in *The Rape of the Lock*—the
gnomes and sylphs and nymphs of Rosicrucianism. The elegant diversity of the poet's material may be suggested by a
random bit from the argument of an early canto of *The
Botanic Garden:*

VIII. The Nymphs of the river Derwent lament the death of Mrs.
French. IX. Inland navigation. Monument for Mr. Brindley. X.
Pumps explained. Child sucking. Mothers exhorted to nurse their
children. Cherub sleeping. XI. Engines for extinguishing fire. Story
of two lovers perishing in the flames. XII. Charities of Miss Jones.
XIII. Marshes drained. Hercules conquers Achilous. The horn of
Plenty.

And so he glides by easy stages into vegetable physiology and
vegetable passions.

The texts of Darwin's poems and his full notes constitute
almost an encyclopaedia of science, but our concern is with
the ideas that make him the great figure between Buffon and
Lamarck; indeed he is justly credited with anticipating Lamarck. At the will of 'God the first cause,' we read in *The*

Temple of Nature, 'Organic Life began beneath the waves' with the 'spontaneous birth' of creatures.

> These, as successive generations bloom,
> New powers acquire, and larger limbs assume.

The oak, whale, lion, eagle, man—who 'styles himself the image of his God'—

> Arose from rudiments of form and sense,
> An embryon point, or microscopic ens.

As land emerged, some creatures of the water became amphibious and new animalcules developed. 'Those situated on dry land, and immersed in dry air, may gradually acquire new powers to preserve their existence; and by innumerable successive reproductions for some thousands, or perhaps millions of ages, may at length have produced many of the vegetable and animal inhabitants which now people the earth.' Darwin censures Buffon and others for thinking 'that mankind arose from one family of monkeys on the banks of the Mediterranean.' We need not pursue his arguments for adaptation to environment (in the Lamarckian or creative sense) in regard to fertilization, protective coloring, the obtaining of food, the transmission of acquired modifications, and so on. And though Darwin may give a general impression of serene deistic optimism, he can picture the struggle for existence— 'And one great Slaughter-house the warring world.' Shelley, we may remember, absorbed much from Darwin, but rather his miscellaneous and utilitarian than his specifically evolutionary ideas, though Darwin's general principles would re inforce Shelley's perfectibilitarian faith.

One important thinker who reacted against Darwin's evolutionary doctrine was Coleridge, a wide reader in science as in everything else. Coleridge criticized Darwin's belief that animals evolved from plants, and maintained the original divergence of the two kinds of organic life. Such a view might have led him on to acceptance of further divergence within species, to evolution, in short, but his scientific and philosophic inclination toward the conception of dynamic continuity was checked by his religious conception of God, nature, and man. Without going into the complications of Coleridge's thought, which have been explored by Professor G. R. Potter, we may illustrate his position by one of his simpler utterances. In 1815 he wrote to Wordsworth about what he had hoped his brother poet would treat in *The Recluse*. First he should remove 'the sandy sophisms of Locke, and the mechanic dogmatists' concerning the senses and the mind.

Next, I understood that you would take the human race in the concrete, have exploded the absurd notion of Pope's 'Essay on Man,' Darwin, and all the countless believers even (strange to say) among Christians of man's having progressed from an orang-outang state —so contrary to all history, to all religion, nay, to all possibility—to have affirmed a Fall in some sense, as a fact, the possibility of which cannot be understood from the nature of the will, but the reality of which is attested by experience and conscience.

As much writing of our own time would suggest, the wisdom behind these remarks cannot be laughed off because of their scientific fallacies.

In the generation before *The Origin of Species,* the English books that made the greatest stir were Sir Charles Lyell's *Principles of Geology* (1830-33) and Robert Chambers' *Vestiges of the Natural History of Creation* (1844). Assembling a mass of data, Lyell rejected the orthodox theory of catastrophic alterations and established in its place the uniformitarian view, already propounded by James Hutton and John Playfair, 'that all former changes of the organic and inorganic creation are referrible to one uninterrupted succession of physical events, governed by the laws now in operation.' Among other things, Lyell stressed the enormous transformations wrought by water, through both erosive action and alluvial deposits—an idea which, like his other ideas, presupposed millions of years, and which inspired some of the finest stanzas of *In Memoriam*. Lyell conducted his argument on the scientific level, but he was aware that his views of the earth's age and of scientific law did not coincide with Genesis and popular assumption; nor did he give warrant for religious optimism concerning man and the universe. Though he was the exponent of gradual geological change, Lyell opposed the growing number of evolutionary theorists. He accepted the idea of man's comparatively recent origin, but found that the evolutionists, notably Lamarck—whose theories Lyell must have introduced to many English readers—had given no evidence for the transmutation of species, for the development of new faculties and organs in response to the demands of environment. Lyell greatly influenced Darwin, and later was converted to belief in Darwinian evolution.

Although our space is limited, I cannot resist quoting a bit from Disraeli's novel *Tancred,* which came out three years after Chambers' *Vestiges:*

After making herself very agreeable, Lady Constance took up a book which was at hand, and said, 'Do you know this?' And Tancred, opening a volume which he had never seen, and then turning to its title-page, found it was 'The Revelations of Chaos,' a startling work just published, and of which a rumour had reached him.

'No,' he replied; 'I have not seen it.'

'I will lend it you if you like: it is one of those books one must read. It explains everything, and is written in a very agreeable style.'

'It explains everything!' said Tancred; 'it must, indeed, be a very remarkable book!'

'I think it will just suit you,' said Lady Constance. 'Do you know, I thought so several times while I was reading it.'

'To judge from the title, the subject is rather obscure,' said Tancred.

'No longer so,' said Lady Constance. 'It is treated scientifically; everything is explained by geology and astronomy, and in that way. It shows you exactly how a star is formed; nothing can be so pretty! A cluster of vapour, the cream of the milky way, a sort of celestial cheese, churned into light, you must read it, 'tis charming.'

'Nobody ever saw a star formed,' said Tancred.

'Perhaps not. You must read the "Revelations"; it is all explained. But what is most interesting, is the way in which man has been developed. You know, all is development. The principle is perpetually going on. First, there was nothing, then there was something; then, I forget the next, I think there were shells, then fishes; then we came, let me see, did we come next? Never mind that; we came at last. And the next change there will be something very superior to us, something with wings. Ah! that's it: we were fishes, and I believe we shall be crows. But you must read it.'

'I do not believe I ever was a fish,' said Tancred.

'Oh! but it is all proved; you must not argue on my rapid sketch; read the book. It is impossible to contradict anything in it. You understand, it is all science; it is not like those books in which one says one thing and another the contrary, and both may be wrong. Everything is proved: by geology, you know. You see exactly how everything is made; how many worlds there have been; how long they lasted; what went before, what comes next. We are a link in the chain, as inferior animals were that preceded us: we in turn shall be inferior; all that will remain of us will be some relics in a new red sandstone. This is development. We had fins; we may have wings.'

That is what happens when science becomes drawing-room news. Chambers, unlike most men, saw a possible degree of truth in Lamarck's theory, even if it was not adequate to explain the origin of species. His own view is that God set creation to evolve by natural law, and that, under favorable conditions, a simple type gave birth to a superior type, and so on, all such advancement proceeding by minute stages. Hence all organic forms, from the humblest lichen to the highest mammal, have a fundamental unity. All inorganic nature is comprehended under the one law of gravitation, all organic life under the one law of development. Chambers' history of the world is summed up in a single sentence: 'The masses of space are formed by law; law makes them in due time theatres of existence for plants and animals; sensation, disposition, intellect, are all in like manner developed and sustained in action by law.' While Chambers has his full share of what was becoming the century's obsessive worship of scientific law, he admits the possibility that man may have been 'specially endowed with an immortal spirit, at the same time that his ordinary mental manifestations are looked upon as simple phenomena resulting from organization. . .' But the concession does not seem whole-hearted, and Chambers can also say:

It is clear, moreover, from the whole scope of the natural laws, that the individual, as far as the present sphere of being is concerned, is to the Author of nature a consideration of inferior moment. Everywhere we see the arrangements for the species perfect; the individual is left, as it were, to take his chance amidst the *mêlée* of the various laws affecting him. If he be found inferiorly endowed, or ill befalls him, there was at least no partiality against him. The system has the fairness of a lottery, in which everyone has the like chance of drawing the prize.

We shall meet this problem in *In Memoriam,* and there are other resemblances. But we are told that the evolutionary sec-

tions of the poem were written before Chambers' book appeared, and indeed the ideas that Tennyson dealt with had
been in the air for some time. One general resemblance, it may
be added, is in the way of long-term optimism, which was
of course a common heritage: Chambers sees man's perpetual
warfare as a natural phase of his early development, which is
only a brief period in the chronology of God.*

We are inclined to associate *In Memoriam* with Tennyson's
middle age, with his marriage, the Laureateship, popularity,
and security, but it is well to remember that it was written
under very different circumstances. If we look at Tennyson in
1833, when he was twenty-four, we see an abnormally sensitive and melancholy young man, lonely, poor, uncertain of the
meaning of life, uncertain also of his own future and of the
poet's place in the modern world. And in that year, as everyone knows, the death of Arthur Hallam brought a profound
personal loss and gave a profound shock to a mind already
much disturbed. Such early poems as *Ulysses* and *Tithonus*
and especially *The Two Voices,* with its explicit opposition
of science and faith, show how close Tennyson came to sui-
cidal despair.

In Memoriam starts from the same question as *Lycidas,*
'How can we maintain belief in God's providence when he
blots out a young life of signal virtue and promise?' But Milton could answer the question with a more assured trust in
God and the ultimate equity of heaven than was possible for
a different kind of man in a modern age, when human history
had become a moment, a pin-point, in time and space and the

* Chambers—that is, the anonymous author of the *Vestiges*—was commonly dismissed or denounced by Victorian scientists as well as laymen
on the ground that he was an unscientific sciolist. He was defended by
Professor Lovejoy in the *Popular Science Monthly,* 75 (1909), 499-514,
537-49.

Creator, for some minds, a mythological footnote to self-sustaining natural law. Tennyson was more akin to Spenser and Donne in his realization of the conflict between belief in a divine order and purpose and acceptance of either mechanistic law or meaningless chaos. The two articles of faith to which he clung were a providential God and human immortality (and he did not share the popular anthropomorphic notion of God as 'an immeasurable clergyman').

The cosmic theme is defined with painful clarity in the third section, where the poet listens to the persuasive voice of Sorrow:

> 'The stars,' she whispers, 'blindly run;
> A web is wov'n across the sky;
> From out waste places comes a cry,
> And murmurs from the dying sun:

> 'And all the phantom, Nature, stands—
> With all the music in her tone,
> A hollow echo of my own,—
> A hollow form with empty hands.'

> And shall I take a thing so blind,
> Embrace her as my natural good;
> Or crush her, like a vice of blood,
> Upon the threshold of the mind?

We are left, for the time, with these naturalistic and religious alternatives.

The question becomes more specific in LV and LVI, where faith in a divine plan and human immortality wrestles with the fact of nature's indifference to the survival not merely of individuals but of whole species:

> Are God and Nature then at strife,
> That Nature lends such evil dreams?

So careful of the type she seems,
So careless of the single life;

That I, considering everywhere
Her secret meaning in her deeds,
And finding that of fifty seeds
She often brings but one to bear . . .

and the poet is reduced to blind hope.* But even species, he
continues, are not preserved.

'So careful of the type?' but no.
From scarped cliff and quarried stone
She cries, 'A thousand types are gone:
I care for nothing, all shall go.'

Is man then only a futile and ephemeral prey of natural
forces?

And he, shall he,

Man, her last work, who seem'd so fair,
Such splendid purpose in his eyes,
Who roll'd the psalm to wintry skies,
Who built him fanes of fruitless prayer,

Who trusted God was love indeed
And love Creation's final law—
Tho' Nature, red in tooth and claw
With ravine, shriek'd against his creed—

---

* We have noticed Chambers' remarks on the insignificance of the
individual in the total scheme, and Tennyson may be remembering
Butler's *Analogy* (Everyman edition, p. 80; H. V. Routh, *Towards the
Twentieth Century*, New York, 1937, p. 86):
'For, of the numerous seeds of vegetables and bodies of animals, which
are adapted and put in the way to improve to such a point or state of
natural maturity and perfection, we do not see perhaps that one in a
million actually does. Far the greatest part of them decay before they
are improved to it, and appear to be absolutely destroyed.'

> Who loved, who suffer'd countless ills,
> Who battled for the True, the Just,
> Be blown about the desert dust,
> Or seal'd within the iron hills?

In thus recoiling from the horrible fact of nature's cruelty (which man has recognized since life began), Tennyson did not, as Professor Lovejoy observed, have the support of the principle of plenitude which the early eighteenth century had so much relied upon to accommodate contradictions—that God was bound to create the fullest variety of existences.

Other moving statements of the central problem might be quoted, but we must turn to Tennyson's answers. Whereas many Victorian readers, scientists among them, seized upon the poem as a triumphant reconciliation of science and religion, it is a cliché of modern criticism that its power is in its dark moods of confusion and despair. The modern view may well be right, though the modern mind is likely to pre-judge the question, and though the poet's affirmations are of such different kinds that they cannot by any means be lumped together for dismissal. Those affirmations may be roughly divided under two headings, the external and the personal. It may be granted that the first heading comprises most of the weak parts of the poem, that Tennyson's effort to relate his faith in a providential God and in immortality to a kind of evolutionary progress on earth was a dubious enterprise, though it was perhaps inevitable at the time and though it would not lack endorsement now. Such a mixture was almost bound to be neither religion nor science but a vague social and ethical optimism, a statement of what the poet wished to believe.

But the affirmations of what with his whole being he did believe move for the most part on another level, because

he had to overcome a terrifying sense of darkness and isolation in a meaningless world.

> And all is well, tho' faith and form
>   Be sunder'd in the night of fear;
>   Well roars the storm to those that hear
> A deeper voice across the storm. . .

Unfortunately that conflict dissolves, in the next stanza, into
social amelioration and the un-British violence of French
revolutionists. For unadulterated personal affirmation we
might turn to the mystical highlight of the poem, the ninety-
fifth section, where, left alone outside as in the house the
symbolic lights go out, the poet feels the immediate presence
of his dead friend and through the power of love has a glimpse
of a reality behind the flux. But sections CXXIII and CXXIV are
closer to our theme:

CXXIII

> There rolls the deep where grew the tree.
>   O earth, what changes hast thou seen!
>   There where the long street roars hath been
> The stillness of the central sea.
>
> The hills are shadows, and they flow
>   From form to form, and nothing stands;
>   They melt like mist, the solid lands,
> Like clouds they shape themselves and go.
>
> But in my spirit will I dwell,
>   And dream my dream, and hold it true;
>   For tho' my lips may breathe adieu,
> I cannot think the thing farewell.

CXXIV

> That which we dare invoke to bless;
>   Our dearest faith; our ghastliest doubt;

He, They, One, All; within, without;
The Power in darkness whom we guess;

I found Him not in world or sun,
    Or eagle's wing, or insect's eye;
    Nor thro' the questions men may try,
The petty cobwebs we have spun:

If e'er when faith had fall'n asleep,
    I heard a voice, 'Believe no more'
    And heard an ever-breaking shore
That tumbled in the Godless deep;

A warmth within the breast would melt
    The freezing reason's colder part,
    And like a man in wrath the heart
Stood up and answer'd, 'I have felt.'

Here Tennyson places man in the midst of endless geological change, rejects—or at least deprecates—the argument from design of the long succession of Paleys, and takes his stand (like Coleridge) on the evidence of his own consciousness. And his position, whether we agree with it or not, seems to me much less vulnerable than it does to many modern readers. The modern reader, I think, shows some inconsistency in these matters. Thomas Hardy's picture of the world may in itself be true or false, but no one complains that that picture, so congenial to our age, is false because it is, like Tennyson's, the subjective vision of the poet, a personal assertion of the unprovable. Yet Tennyson, who sees a world quite as bleak as Hardy's, and who in a very real struggle maintains his version of the unprovable, is somehow guilty of the well-known Victorian habit of self-deception from which our minds are so happily free.

We have been considering Tennyson's general reaction, not

his precise scientific ideas, but, since those ideas are sometimes vaguely thought of as anticipations of Darwin, we may
observe that he was not concerned with the central Darwinian
doctrine of the mutation of species. That doctrine was held,
as we have seen, by some pre-Darwinian theorists, among them
Herbert Spencer, but the chief scientists of the age, who were
Tennyson's chief guides, believed in nature's successive pro-
duction of higher forms of life, not in organic evolution. That
partly optimistic belief was apparently fused, in Tennyson's
mind, with other and older ideas of progress. But his questionings turn on the immensity of the celestial system, the
timeless process of geological change, the wasteful productivity
and destructiveness of nature, and the struggle for existence,
as these grim facts bear upon the doubtful place and destiny
of man and the whole problem of religious faith. Such scientific concepts were later to be bound up with Darwinism,
but all of them except the geological process were as old as
human thought. Although Tennyson was a closer student of
science than other poets, his concern was with man and God
rather than with particular scientific theories. And *In Memoriam* did not put an end to his study of science or the problems
of his mind and soul. When *The Origin of Species* came out,
he was prepared to accept it, so far as it went, though he recoiled from the naturalistic implications of Darwinism.

We cannot look at Tennyson's other poems and we can
take only a squint at the likewise voluminous Browning. For
both, science—and religion also—had killed the Wordsworthian view of nature. Their religious faith, if not quite orthodox, was founded on a God of love working in some way
through imperfect creation and fulfilling human potentialities in another life. We have seen that Tennyson's creed was
hardly facile; whether or not Browning's was remains more
of a question. At any rate the chief articles of their faith had

become impossible for two poets only ten or twelve years younger, Matthew Arnold and his friend Clough.

To illustrate the change of climate, we might put Browning's *Paracelsus* (1835) beside Arnold's *Empedocles on Etna* (1852). The young Browning, a fervent disciple of Shelley, dramatized the limited vision, and the failure, of both Paracelsus, the aspiring scientist, and Aprile, the idealistic poet. The scientist has sought to know as the poet to love, the former excluding love and the latter knowledge; each seems to be the half of a dissevered whole. But the whole, Browning insists, is really far greater than those imperfect parts. His conception of knowledge and love goes beyond both scientific mastery of the finite and romantic yearning for the infinite; it is based on surrender to the divine love that stoops to lift frail and finite man. Hence the dying Paracelsus learns that a higher and humbler kind of knowledge and love must go together in man, that the God of power and love

> dwells in all,
> From life's minute beginnings, up at last
> To man—the consummation of this scheme
> Of being, the completion of this sphere
> Of life;

that progress is 'The law of life, man is not Man as yet'; and that the aspiring mind and soul must have fulfilment 'in some better sphere.' Browning was, and remained, a spiritual evolutionist, in the upward connotation of the term, but, while he later took some cognizance of Darwin, he had little of Tennyson's anxious concern with science and went on in his own way.

Fourteen years after *Paracelsus*, and the year before *In Memoriam*, Matthew Arnold surprised his family and friends by putting forth a volume of poems in which the sophisti-

cated young dandy revealed himself as a lonely, troubled soul
who turned away from the distracting world to grope after
truth and order. Cut off—though the son of a notable religious leader—from traditional faith, and feeling isolated in
an empty universe, the serious young idealist could not accept
life as a meaningless chaos or himself as a mere bundle of discordant impulses. If he was to rise above shallow busyness
or sterile naturalism or blank despair, he must, in Stoic fashion, achieve law and order within himself and see a purpose
in life larger and higher than himself. Most of Arnold's poems,
then and later, were variations on this general theme. In his
fullest statement of the problem, *Empedocles on Etna,* he
presented a scientific thinker who, though he has no Para-
celsian vision of man's ascent to God, does, like Paracelsus,
recognize the true wholeness of man's nature. But he is driven
to suicide by his restless, devouring intellect, which has become his whole being and has killed his capacity for simple,
natural feeling and joy. This Wordsworthian capacity is represented by the young Callicles, as the Shelleyan Aprile represented poetry and love; but whereas Aprile was an instrument
of Paracelsus' inspiring revelation, the songs of Callicles only
remind Empedocles of his fatal loss. In other words, Browning
achieved a characteristic fusion of the head and the heart;
Arnold sees only an irreconcilable split.

We cannot go into the complexities of Arnold's melancholy
predicament, though his poetic account of it, at least on its
negative side, has remained more acceptable to the modern
temper than that of any other Victorian poet. The general
causes are clear enough—his recoil from a bustling world of
mechanical progress and shallow or sordid aims, his religious
skepticism and sense of disintegration and rootlessness, the
internal conflicts (partly involved in his love for Marguerite)
between the claims of instinctive emotion and those of rigor-

ous self-discipline. An idealism which had no outlet in orthodox religion was unsatisfied by Stoic austerity. While the mass
of men unthinkingly pursue their worldly ends, for the intellectual the healthy, happy balance of mind and feeling has
been upset by the pressure of modern thought. Arnold would
not—or not very often—escape from or repudiate the intellectual responsibilities of modern man, but he would if possible
revive man's natural roots. He would call up memories of the
old world to redress the balance of the new. The feverish modern mind may be healed and refreshed by contemplating the
simple rightness of feeling that Arnold sees in the biblical
or the classical past, or by contemplating the ultimate peace
and Neoplatonic unity of being often symbolized in his poems
—as in *Intimations of Immortality*—by the sea. To this partial
anti-intellectualism belongs Arnold's Wordsworthian nostalgia. As Wordsworth, reacting against both Godwinism and
commercialism, appealed to the goodness of nature or the
natural religion of the Greeks, so Arnold invoked Wordsworth
as the

> priest to us all
> Of the wonder and bloom of the world.

Wordsworth had recognized the need of natural feeling, and
himself had shed

> On spirits that had long been dead,
> Spirits dried up and closely-furl'd,
> The freshness of the early world.

Yet Wordsworth had averted his gaze 'From half of human
fate,' and his creed would hardly sustain modern man, least
of all the poet who could say:

> Nature, with equal mind,
> Sees all her sons at play;

Sees man control the wind,
The wind sweep man away.

Arnold was in quest of an idea of unity and totality which he
found wanting in Tennyson and Browning, Keats and Shelley,
and the quest itself carried some poetic alleviations for spiritual trouble. Moreover, if the poet died, the school-inspector,
the Stoic moralist, the literary, political, and religious critic
took his place. And the later Arnold was more and more to
stress conduct as three fourths of life, morality nourished by
humane letters and poetry and a rational religion, with the
intellectual sanctions of science.

Arnold's friend Clough, who died in 1861 at the age of
forty-two, found no solution except in the Carlylean gospel of
work and duty and loyalty to a stern ideal of truth. He had a
more positive reverence for the scientific spirit than Arnold,
though not when that spirit became mechanistic. The contrast
between the age of primitive faith and the age of scientific
rationalism is plainly, not to say prosaically, stated in *The
New Sinai:*

> And as of old from Sinai's top
>   God said that God is One,
> By Science strict so speaks He now
>   To tell us, There is None!
> Earth goes by chemic forces; Heaven's
>   A Mécanique Céleste!
> And heart and mind of human kind
>   A watch-work as the rest!

We have not much evidence about the scientific reading
done by Arnold and Clough, though Clough's reference to
Laplace is one item, and though he seems, in *Natura Naturans*
(1849), to espouse a rather vague idea of biological development. The physical sciences doubtless contributed to the nega-

tions that weighed upon both men, but probably more important was the newest branch of science, rationalistic criticism of the Bible and the traditional creed. Especially from the eighteen-thirties onward, there was a stream of such books. One English pioneer was Charles Hennell, the friend of the young Marian Evans, and she herself—with an image of Christ hanging before her—toiled at translating the most famous early work of higher criticism, that of Strauss, who took the gospel narratives in terms of religious myth or symbolism. Carlyle, on the one hand the mystical and inspiring prophet of anti-rationalism, on the other hand was a railer against 'Hebrew Old Clothes.' Carlyle's future biographer, James Anthony Froude, brother of a leader of the Oxford Movement, wrote *The Nemesis of Faith* (1849). In 1850, five years after Newman went over to Rome, his brother Francis published *Phases of Faith,* an account of his own arrival at skepticism. In 1860 *Essays and Reviews,* by a group of liberals (all but one clergymen) who became known as the 'Seven against Christ,' led to a trial and to Lord Westbury's dismissing hell with costs and taking away from orthodox members of the Church of England their last hope of everlasting damnation. Hard upon that episode followed the notorious work and misfortunes of the well-meaning Bishop Colenso. And in 1863 came Renan's *Life of Jesus,* the chief successor to Strauss's book. One must be very wanting in imagination if one does not sympathize at least as much with the conservatives as with the iconoclasts.

Clough, who dealt with the problem of belief in a good many poems, clung himself to some kind of shadowy divinity, in the soul of man or in Truth. To quote the beginning and end of his *Epi-Strauss-ium,*

> Matthew and Mark and Luke and holy John
> Evanished all and gone! . . .

However,
The place of worship the meantime with light
Is, if less richly, more sincerely bright,
And in blue skies the Orb is manifest to sight.

Browning was much more hostile than Clough to Strauss and higher criticism in general. If we had time we could follow his reactions through many poems, beginning with *Christmas-Eve and Easter-Day* (1850). Browning could not take historical criticism as final, because human reason and knowledge are limited and fallible and because the real evidence is within the soul. He sees the divinity of Christ and the transforming power of human and divine love as facts of experience which mere biblical scholarship cannot overthrow. Thus, in spite of his antagonism to Strauss, Browning's attitude was not altogether different, though his positive faith was less intellectual and more fervent. In opposition to both ritualism and the skepticism of Renan, he declares, in the *Epilogue* to *Dramatis Personae* (1864):

That one Face, far from vanish, rather grows,
Or decomposes but to recompose,
Become my universe that feels and knows.

This volume contained that great satire on anthropomorphic ideas of God, *Caliban upon Setebos,* which probably started from Browning's reading of Darwin, and which brings us back to biology. We must, however, take for granted both *The Origin of Species* and the controversy that followed it. This was, on a more reverberating scale, a continuation of the debate that, stimulated by Lyell and Chambers, had been going on for decades. The central scientific issue had been whether new species had come into being by mutation or by special creation; each theory explained the known facts and each had a large element of faith. Darwin's achievement was

to bring a new weight of evidence in support of mutation
and to supply a plausible theory of its method of working, a
theory which was of course purely naturalistic. It has often
been said or assumed, by people who see only Bishop Wilber-
force and Huxley in the Oxford arena, that the first battle
over Darwinism was between clear-headed scientists and thick-
headed Fundamentalists. It most assuredly was not. Some the-
ologians were on Darwin's side, and arrayed against him were
the majority of scientists, such leaders as Sir Richard Owen,
Adam Sedgwick, and Louis Agassiz and many lesser men. And
opponents were moved by scientific reasons as well as by preju-
dice or religious convictions. In time, thanks in part to Huxley's vigorous propaganda, the doctrine of evolution was established; and, though Darwin's explanation of the process later
fell into disrepute, nowadays natural selection seems to have
returned to a place of prime importance in the biological
picture. About the causes and ends of evolution scientists in
general do not ask.

The Origin of Species and The Descent of Man (1871) inaugurated a way of thought that has changed our whole outlook, and we can only touch on the religious and ethical implications. In 1859 Adam Sedgwick, who has lived in fame
chiefly as an opponent of evolution, wrote to Darwin protest-
ing that the Darwinian theory ignored, and attempted to
sever, the link between the material and the moral and religious:

Were it possible (which, thank God, it is not) to break it, humanity,
in my mind, would suffer a damage that might brutalize it, and
sink the human race into a lower grade of degradation than any
into which it has fallen since its written records tell us of its history.

(These words are quoted, I may add, by Geoffrey West in his
biography of Darwin as a 'prophecy fulfilled to-day with a

strange and terrible fatality.' *) In the long tradition of classical-Christian thought, man had been linked as an animal
with animals, but also, and primarily, as a rational mind and
immortal spirit with God. In a strictly biological and naturalistic account of growth, strife, and waste there seemed to be
little room for God the Creator and Designer, still less for God
the Father, or for man as a being of God-like soul. On the
other hand, it was possible for the non-Christian idealist to
find strength and hope in the thought of man's emergence
from the jungle or his ascent from the protoplasm.

These negative and positive attitudes are represented with
antithetical clarity by the two novelist-poets, Hardy and Meredith. For Meredith the doctrine of evolution was a challenge
and an inspiration, both ethical and social. Man must accept
the basic fact that he is an animal, but his senses, his animal
energies, must be ruled by brain and spirit if he is to realize
his human potentialities. And the individual must ally himself with the creative purpose in the world and take his share
in the progressive improvement of the race. This ethical psychology may recall that of some Renaissance humanists, the
Stoic George Chapman in particular, with Christianity left
out. Meredith's strenuous optimism has been under a cloud
during the last thirty years, and during the same period the
pessimism of his mighty opposite has been in high favor. The
contrast between them might be illustrated by two poems
which happen to be identical in their nominal theme. In *The
Thrush in February* (1885), Meredith characteristically rejoices in man's being a conscious and happy instrument of a
continuing purpose; he feels 'The rapture of the forward

* Geoffrey West, *Charles Darwin* (London: Routledge, 1937, p. 317;
Yale University Press, 1938, p. 325). See John W. Clark and T. McK.
Hughes, *The Life and Letters of the Reverend Adam Sedgwick* (Cambridge
University Press, 1890), II, 357.

view.' In *The Darkling Thrush,* written in December 1900, Hardy surveys a bleak winter landscape that looks like the century's corpse, while

> An aged thrush, frail, gaunt, and small,
>   In blast-beruffled plume,

pours forth a song so joyful that it seems to be inspired by

> Some blessed hope, whereof he knew
>   And I was unaware.*

The intellectual ideas of the self-educated Hardy—if not his imagination and compassion—started from such emancipators as Mill, Darwin, Spencer, and *Essays and Reviews.* And although his poetic fame and much of his writing belonged to his old age and the twentieth century, his outlook had undergone little or no change since it had been set forth in 1866, in the grim sonnet *Hap.* Moreover, his anti-religious fatalism was much like that of Swinburne's *Atalanta in Calydon* and *Poems and Ballads* of 1865-6 and of FitzGerald's earlier *Rubáiyát,* though Hardy wore no Hellenic or Persian costume but his own homespun, and though his voice was quieter and sadder. There is no need of citing the poems in which he pictured a universe made by some vast Imbecility or a Godhead dying downwards, or in which he offered the faint hope that eventually consciousness might inform the Immanent Will. Both Hardy's matter and his manner proved welcome to the early decades of our century, and his philosophy appeared to have a special scientific sanction. Yet it is, as I said before, no less personal and intuitive a reading of life than Tennyson's, or Meredith's. If a scientist or positivist

* From Thomas Hardy, *Collected Poems* (copyright 1925 by The Macmillan Company). Used by permission.

should say 'So much the worse for intuition,' one could only answer that science cannot solve the chief questions man asks, whether they belong to metaphysics or to everyday life.

As for the later Victorian age in general, we have observed some effects of astronomy, geology, biology, and biblical criticism upon traditional Christianity, and these effects widened and deepened as time went on. It is easier for us than it was for many Victorians to see that much of what crumbled under the pressure of science was rather the adventitious accretions of religion, such as the scientific validity of Genesis, than religion itself. And we tend to forget, as people did then, that supposedly infallible dogmas of science were crumbling too. There was, moreover, a great gain in the application of historical and evolutionary concepts to theology and religion. Yet science and higher criticism did menace the specific doctrines of Christianity and the basis of any kind of theism. Matthew Arnold in his later years devoted earnest effort to saving what seemed to be essential in Christianity from what threatened to be a general wreckage; he sought to do so by making the Bible 'poetical' and religion verifiable. Many other writers embraced the secular 'religion of humanity'; and many poets worshiped only at the aesthetic altar, though some of them ended in the church. Late Victorian rationalism, nourished by the century's rigorous faith in scientific law, could be no less dogmatic, and much more arid, than Fundamentalism. For a picture of a state of mind fairly widespread then, and now, one might quote H. G. Wells, himself a product of science and the religion of humanity. He is describing, under a transparent alias, Edward Clodd (who was, incidentally, a friend of Hardy and of Meredith):

Dodd is a leading member of the Rationalist Press Association, a militant agnostic, and a dear, compact man, one of those Middle

Victorians who go about with a preoccupied, caulking air, as though, after having been at great cost and pains to banish God from the Universe, they were resolved not to permit Him back on any terms whatever. He has constituted himself a sort of alert customs officer of a materialistic age . . . examining every proposition to see that the Creator wasn't being smuggled back under some specious new generalization. Boon used to declare that every night Dodd looked under his bed for the Deity, and slept with a large revolver under his pillow for fear of a revelation.*

I am reminded of an old Harvard anecdote that President Conant revived a while ago. Members of the department of philosophy chose for a new building the inscription, 'Man is the measure of all things,' and went away for the summer; when they came back, the inscription, having passed under President Eliot's eye, had become 'What is man that Thou art mindful of him?'

We might end this rapid survey by registering an emphatic protest against a habit that may have declined somewhat of late years but is by no means dead, that of regarding the Victorians as smugly optimistic. Persons who do thus condemn or patronize the Victorians only betray a large ignorance of the period and a smugness based on no very clear evidence of modern superiority. That throughout the Victorian age a great many people had a complacent belief in progress is no doubt true, as it is of the same kind of people nowadays; but how many of the great and less great Victorian poets, novelists, and critics can be named who shared that belief? If the name of Macaulay leaps to mind, is there anything in him that approaches, for example, this sentence from the well-known liberal and champion of science, Horace M. Kallen?

* *Boon* (New York: Doran, 1915), pp. 46-7. By permission of Mrs. M. Wells. The *D.N.B.* for 1922-30, by the way, denies that Clodd was militant.

In terms of their consequences to the health, the comfort, the security, and the joy of life, the labors of men like Pasteur or Watt or Faraday or Edison or Ford have earned better at the hands of mankind than the labors of men like Jesus or Moses or Buddha or Mohammed.*

A roll-call of Victorian authors would indicate, along with a wide variety of particular reactions, an almost unanimous pessimism, of hues ranging from gray to black. Perhaps the chief difference between them and many moderns is that the Victorians were less inclined to stew in despair. And if it be said that their efforts to find a way out were unsatisfactory, what have ours been?

* 'The Warfare of Religion Against Science,' *The Liberal Spirit* (Cornell University Press, 1948), p. 119.

VI

Modern Science and Modern Poetry

The poets whose maturity has fallen within the past thirty or forty years have felt the pressure of most of the problems of earlier times, along with all that our century has added to the demonstration of scientific power and human inadequacy, including the convulsions and consequences of two world wars. In trying to indicate the background or climate of modern poetry, in the broad terms befitting the last chapter of our story, it is even less possible than before to avoid outlining the obvious, omitting much that is significant, and saying things with unqualified brevity. The problems are numerous and complex, but some of the major ones might be grouped under two headings, the failure of belief and the estrangement of the artist from society. The two questions are related to each other and both are related to science. Although the second grows in part out of the first, we shall begin with it.

From antiquity through the Renaissance and beyond, the serious poet was considered, and considered himself, a teacher and leader of his fellows; but he was also, like Dante or Shakespeare or Milton, a man among men, a citizen among citizens, sharing the common experience and outlook. The alienation of the poet from society—though it is in some sense as old as literature—seems to have been first felt as a real problem in the romantic age. We have seen that the romantic poets did not share either the religious creed professed by the mass of people or the rationalistic creed of scientific intellectuals. Moreover, the world inaugurated by the Industrial Revolution was founded on values antagonistic to those of the artist. Throughout the nineteenth century the social critics and novelists and some poets were exposing the enormous human cost of 'progress'; but during the second half—while Arnold was saying that modern poetry must take over the responsibilities of religion—a good many minor poets were seeking refuge in the ivory tower of aestheticism, above the sordid world of the acquisitive, Philistine bourgeoisie.

In our century (and especially in the past thirty-five years), though poetry has again developed an active social conscience, the accelerated operation of the old causes, with new ones added, has separated the artist still further from mankind at large. The relative cultural homogeneity of earlier ages, which has been breaking down for generations, has become a chaos of molecular or atomic diversity. The rapid growth of professionalized knowledge has made even a university faculty a collection of mutually repellent particles. There seems to be no central and traditional community of experience and outlook which the poet can share and use. Nor does there seem to be much room for him in the modern industrial, scientific, militaristic, and culturally vulgarized world. In short, the man among men, the citizen among citizens, has become a detached, isolated, hostile observer of society.

Partly for such reasons, the internal evolution of poetry has widened the gulf between the writer and potential readers. The past thirty years or so have produced a large body of verse that is notoriously difficult. The poet has felt, not without cause, that the still small voice is not heard and not wanted in the modern literary market-place, and that an artist of integrity has no choice but to write for the comparatively small group of the elect. Such a cleavage between the poet and the general public is unfortunate for both parties. No modern poem can have, or at least has had, the wide impact of *In Memoriam,* for instance; and, granted that much of Tennyson's writing was damaged by his popularity, one may doubt if that hurt him more than esotericism has hurt modern poetry and impaired its influence.

Poets have naturally reacted against obvious simplicity and obvious didacticism and have said that poetry written in the modern world cannot help being obscure. That is largely true, no doubt, and to question its entire truth is to brand oneself a naive outsider. I will say none the less that I think the chaos of the modern mind has expressed itself in a good deal of quite insignificant experimentalism in all the arts, and not merely on the lunatic fringe, and that good poets can be charged with some degree of artificial and conventional obscurity. Conscious of uncertainty in all the supposedly eternal verities, the moderns have outlawed direct expression of ideas and emotion and have insisted on the oblique and often ironic presentation of immediate perceptions and particular images, with little or none of the explaining and reflecting that traditional poetry provides. In this great change scientific skepticism and scientific objectivity, even the partial breakdown of old scientific notions of regular continuity in nature, have had their considerable share. And a poetic texture of objective and complex discontinuity and particularity, often based on the free association of more or less private symbols and drawing on the heterogeneous storehouse of the unconscious, does not assist communication. Further, modern poets have learned their technique from such various sources as Dante, Donne, the French Symbolists, and the internal-combustion engine, and in general—with exceptions, of course—they have turned away from nineteenth-century poetry as too 'poetical.' They themselves have aimed at colloquial speech and rhythms, though this colloquialism can at times be as unnatural as any previous poetic idiom. Thus we have the at least superficially paradoxical situation that the 'poetical' Victorians had a popular audience and the colloquial moderns have not. On the whole, if poetry is nowadays less of a force in civilization than it has been (and it would be hard to prove otherwise), the chief fault is in the quality of our civilization; but I think also that some guilt lies with the poets, who have too readily given up the effort to reach a general audience and have been too content to write for one another and for the critics who have rationalized their retreat. It may be added that some of the younger poets—I do not refer to Dylan Thomas or William Empson—have shown signs of a return to lucidity and order.

To come to our second topic, the failure of belief, it is plain that romantic and Victorian idealism, if not entirely dead in the soul of modern man and modern poets, has at least been driven to negative or disguised expression—though many intellectuals and humanitarians nowadays remain good nineteenth-century liberals. But the great phenomenon of our time has been the common decay of religious faith and of religious sanctions for morality. While anti-religious skepticism and naturalism have of course been present in human thought from the beginning, what marks the later nineteenth and especially the twentieth century has been the rapid extension of such attitudes, on philosophic or unphilosophic levels, among an intelligentsia vastly widened through modern education. (The reference to education is purely quantitative, not qualitative.) We cannot overestimate the significance of the common change, in the lifetime of many of us, from belief in a providential God of love, in immortality, in the religious conscience and sin, in the whole Christian creed, to acceptance of the natural man and his scientifically known world as the only realities, a world in which—as Stephen Spender has said —man has no soul to be either saved or damned. To many moderns that may seem the long-delayed advent of a new era in which man can go forward unshackled by a mythological past. The poet, and man in general, might ask what, if the religious quest is not a main object in the human adventure, we are to go forward to—a utopia of gadgets, a heaven of abstract cerebration, 'a scientific morality,' or universal destruction?

It is obvious that the nineteenth and twentieth centuries have immensely enlarged human knowledge in all directions, from the atom and the cell to the astronomical universe, and that there has been, as always, a corresponding enlargement of human ignorance. It is also obvious that the common failure of belief, and failure of nerve, have been to no small degree a direct or indirect result of science (though it is an even clearer fact that scientific rationalism has not been fatal for a considerable number of educated Chriştians, including a few scientists). But, while taking some central things for granted, we must, as in looking at earlier periods, remind ourselves of some of the particular effects of science.

The direction of astronomical discovery might be suggested by two memorable quatrains. The first—whose author I do not know—is a bed time verse for the modern child:

> Twinkle, twinkle, little star,
> I don't wonder what you are,
> For by the spectroscopic ken
> I know that you are hydrogen.

The other is Sir John Squire's *In Continuation of Pope on Newton:**

> Nature and Nature's laws lay hid in night:
> God said, 'Let Newton be!' and all was light.

*'In Continuation of Pope on Newton,' *Collected Poems of Sir John Squire* (London: Macmillan & Co., Ltd., 1959) . Used by permission of Macmillan & Co., Ltd., and Mr. Raglan Squire.

> It did not last: the Devil howling 'Ho,
> Let Einstein be,' restored the status quo.

We have seen how, in the early seventeenth century, old ideas along with new discoveries dismayed some men, and how Donne, Milton, and others urged the primacy of the religious life over external speculation; how in the early eighteenth century Newton made the universe again a divine order which poets could acclaim; how in the early nineteenth century poets revolted against Newtonian mechanism; and how Tennyson struggled to maintain his faith in immortality and a God above measureless space and time. Although to Arnold and Meredith the ordered movements of the stars exemplified the silent, joyful performance of duty, the army of unalterable law, the modern mind has been more disposed, like the neurotic hero of *Maud,* to see the stars as

> Innumerable, pitiless, passionless eyes,
> Cold fires, yet with power to burn and brand
> His nothingness into man.

In 1902, at the end of the last book he published before his death, Herbert Spencer confessed the horror with which he shrank from contemplating the 'Great Enigma' of space, space which had no beginning and can have no end, and 'compared with which our immeasurable sidereal system dwindles to a point.' In the same year Bertrand Russell wrote his well-known essay, 'A Free Man's Worship.' He saw man as the product of one of the numberless fragments thrown off into space by a blind, omnipotent Nature, and human hopes and fears, loves and beliefs, as only the outcome of accidental collocations of atoms. In this scientific parallel, in over-wrought prose, to Swinburne's *Prelude* and Henley's *Invictus,* man was allowed the freedom to worship his heroic and stoic self.

Hardly less depressing, perhaps, than these stark pronouncements was the account of general scientific and metaphysical skepticism and confusion that was being set down about the same time by Henry Adams, in some chapters of his *Education*. Even though mechanistic doctrines of the nineteenth century came to be repudiated, the new and more fluid conceptions were not much more reassuring, and the staggering fact of immensity or infinity has remained a part of the modern consciousness. Bertrand Russell's picture might be said to have reappeared, for instance, in a paper of 1948 entitled 'Man's Greatest Illusion,' by a distinguished historian, Robert L. Schuyler.* The illusion is man's traditional belief in his cosmic importance. Appealing to the inconceivable magnitude of the modern astronomical universe as a corrective to human arrogance, Professor Schuyler urges historically minded humility. We might find a more authentic kind of humility, a wisdom deeper than that of astro-physics, in four lines of Robert Frost:

> They cannot scare me with their empty spaces
> Between stars—on stars where no human race is.
> I have it in me so much nearer home
> To scare myself with my own desert places.†

Such an attitude may remind us of Chapman and Greville and other early poets of the humanistic tradition.

To turn to modern biology, evolution being universally accepted, there remains—apart from many scientific problems—the prime question of its being purposive or purposeless; and the question includes not merely organic life on this

---

* See above, p. 29, note.

†From 'Desert Places' in *Complete Poems of Robert Frost*. Copyright 1936 by Robert Frost. Copyright © 1964 by Lesley Frost Ballantine. Reprinted by permission of Holt, Rinehart and Winston, Inc., and Jonathan Cape. Ltd.

earth but the whole physical universe and the spiritual constitution and destiny of man. Skeptical and 'agnostic' answers seem to come from most scientists, who usually dislike attempts at philosophic interpretation of scientific data. But it may be said that the fact of man's animality has become as fixed and dominant in the modern habit of mind as belief in his rationality and spirituality was throughout earlier ages, and that has imposed a heavy handicap upon any kind of ethical or religious idealism.* Cicero, the great humanist and teacher of humanism, in *De Officiis* (I. iv. 11) distinguished the beast, which lives only in its senses and the moment, from man, who, because he is endowed with reason, sees the connection of cause and effect, draws analogies, relates present and future, and thus can order the course of his life. By way of measuring the progress of two thousand years, we might recall an early poem of Aldous Huxley's, written before he had arrived at complete loathing of the human race and its scientific progress. Mr. Huxley pictured man as 'A poor degenerate from the ape,' superior only in the powers of mind that enable him to explore metaphysics and discover analogies—'Mind fabulous, mind sublime and free!'

> But oh, the sound of simian mirth!
> Mind, issued from the monkey's womb,
> Is still umbilical to earth,
> Earth its home and earth its tomb.†

Earth here is not George Meredith's bountiful and beneficent mother of 'her great venture, Man.' And we might remember

---

* Mr. Frost is too expensive to quote, but one might refer to his poem *The White-tailed Hornet* for a pregnant condensation of modern spiritual and literary history.

† 'First Philosopher's Song,' *Leda* (London: Chatto and Windus: New York: Doran, 1920); *Verses & A Comedy* (London: Chatto and Windus, 1946). Used by permission.

the words quoted before from Adam Sedgwick's earnest letter to Darwin. To come back to Aldous Huxley, whatever our view of his own later evolution, we may think that he has seen further than his brother, Thomas Huxley's other grandson. Julian Huxley the biologist remains a confident evolutionist who knows all the answers—for example, that all intuitive theories of ethics may now be ruled out, since the conscience originates in the infant's conflict between love and hate for its mother.

The undermining of traditional moral values, which has gone along with scientific *hybris,* has been very largely assisted by anthropology and psychology. It has been taught on all sides of late—though the idea itself is very old—that the highest conceptions of religion and ethics that man has attained are only tribal tabus and tribal *mores,* and they have been scientifically sacrificed on the altar of cultural relativity. Without asking how far this general doctrine, like Julian Huxley's explanation of the conscience, involves the 'fallacy of origins,' we can say briefly that the science of anthropology takes its stand on the dogma 'Whatever is is right.' Of course anthropologists have humanitarian aims, and the problems of our society are constantly being illuminated by reports on the manners and morals of aborigines.

Then the spiritual vacuum left in modern man was very quickly filled by Freudian psychology, an account of the human body and spirit which carried Freud's own obsessions and limitations. Though much of Freud has been rejected or broadened by other psychologists, it was mainly Freudian psychology (and behaviorism) that took hold of modern literature and the popular mind. Whatever the therapeutic ends of Freud and his fellows, the common effect of psychology was to encourage the surrender of the conscious, rational, ethical self to the forces of the unconscious. The substantial, self-directing personality became a strip of film recording chaotic sensations and responding automatically to chaotic impulses —as we may see in much modern fiction. The lengths to which psychological and sociological determinism can go might be illustrated by an assertion made to a gathering of prison officials—that the idea that man is responsible for his behavior belongs to the age of witchcraft; one might suggest, following the speaker's own logic, that he was not responsible for what he said. In any case, the very existence of psychiatry and the widespread reliance upon it is in itself a sufficient proof of widespread disease. I can only mention Freud's theory of art as wish-fulfilment, neurotic fantasy engendered by frustration —the scientist's view of escape from reality which we met long ago in Bacon.

Man has always lived by religious, ethical, metaphysical, and aesthetic ideals above himself, however far he has fallen short of them, and until modern times these have had as a rule the endorsement of philosophic authority. If we ask what philosophy now offers man in his confusion and hunger, one answer might be 'Not bread but a stone.' The dominant thinking of our time, whatever its particular label, has been more or less a pragmatic rationalization of surrender to nature and immediacy, to science, in short. The queen of the sciences and humanities has sat down meekly at the door of the laboratory to pick up what fragments of empirical truth may be thrown out. Nowadays one is quite out of date unless one regards as unverifiable, and therefore meaningless, the ideals and concepts of man's age-old search for wisdom and direction. To be sure, the positivist, as the austere and infallible exponent of truth, might say to the questioner, 'I am not bound to please thee with my answers'; but neither are we bound to accept as oracles the Gradgrinds of philosophy.

A number of readers, I am aware, may by this time have been inflamed to the point of incandescence; these remarks, however, are not offered as a rounded sketch of modern science and thought. The nature of our theme, all along, has focused our attention not upon the services of science to truth and man, which the poet like everyone else thankfully welcomes, but upon the liabilities and negations, apparent or real, that scientific progress has entailed. We may remember, too, that the history of scientific progress includes the history of scientific error, the exploding of many scientific claims and dogmas. At any rate I have only tried to catalogue some of the ways in which science has deprived modern man of his spiritual heritage, and the evidence is everywhere in poetry and criticism—for example, in such specific documents as Auden's *New Year Letter* and Karl Shapiro's *Essay on Rime*. The decline of faith in religion and in reason, the general breakdown of values, the skeptical distrust of everything except the pragmatic fact; the isolation of the individual from his fellows and from the past; the contrast between material advance and the quality of life; the mechanization of everyday existence, and even of the mind and the heart, to a degree undreamed of before; the development of scientific power which has made the annihilation of the race a conceivable and perhaps desirable event—all this and more has created a sense of outward and inward insecurity, rootlessness, and emptiness which has probably been more widely felt and more paralyzing than any comparable 'enlightenment' of earlier times. As Max Horkheimer says, in his *Eclipse of Reason* (1947), the theme of our age is self-preservation, while there is no self to preserve. To quote Mr. Auden, whose evolution has been perhaps the fullest single epitome of the modern spirit's journeyings,

                    I mean
That the world of space where events re-occur is still there,
Only now it's no longer real; the real one is nowhere
Where time never moves and nothing can ever happen:
I mean that although there's a person we know all about
Still bearing our name and loving himself as before,
That person has become a fiction; our true existence
Is decided by no one and has no importance to love.

    That is why we despair; that is why we would welcome
The nursery bogey or the winecellar ghost, why even
The violent howling of winter and war has become
Like a juke-box tune that we dare not stop. We are afraid
Of pain but more afraid of silence; for no nightmare
Of hostile objects could be as terrible as this Void.
This is the Abomination. This is the wrath of God.*

In speaking of the difficulty of modern poetry, I remarked that we must distinguish, if we can, between authentic obscurity and mere fashion; and—though it is not correct to say so—I think we must make a parallel distinction between authentic pessimism (if one may use a crude word) and a fashionable cult of despair. It would be possible to argue that a good deal of modern poetry has done more to heighten and propagate despair than to provide spiritual leadership (if one may use a phrase calculated to outrage poets and their critical sponsors). Every warbler has had the tune by heart. And there has been rather too much indulgence in self-pity. Such self-pity has grown partly, to be sure, out of the grim actualities of man's and the poet's situation; but it has grown partly, too, out of a dubious nostalgia, an idealized notion of the past as favorable to the spiritual and heroic life and to poetry. All

*Copyright 1944 by W. H. Auden. Reprinted from 'For the Time Being' in *Collected Poetry of W. H. Auden*, by permission of Random House, Inc., and Faber and Faber, Ltd.

times have been 'damned times,' as Arnold said a hundred years ago of his age.

Whatever may be thought about those questions, it is certain that poetry must be the product of the whole being; it is an act of integrity and faith, and it cannot live on either surface evasions or on a merely negative skepticism which reduces life and man to shadows in a cave. And the poetic imagination, now as always, requires myth, those basic fables and symbols, evolved by the racial consciousness and enriched by racial and poetic transmission, that embody the spiritual realities by which man has lived. But the climate of the modern world, the mechanized chaos of the modern city, can only blight that kind of myth and the modes of natural and communal experience it represents—as the romantic writers and the young Tennyson foresaw. The modern poetic revolt against scientific positivism has some obvious similarities to the romantic revolt against Newtonian mechanism, but modern poets have recognized the inadequacy of romanticism partly through being deprived by science of some central elements of the romantic faith. All modern poetry has been conditioned by science, even those areas that seem farthest removed from it. And though modern poets have been united in revolt against the positivistic and mechanistic habit of mind and the world it has created, they have of course revolted in very different ways and directions. Some have been quoted already, and we can look only at a few eminent and diverse representatives of conscious and direct reaction.

First, however, we must glance backward at some earlier American writers, partly on their own account and partly in order to appreciate the change of temper in recent poetry. Until this past generation, American poets were in the main disposed to accept the universe. The conflict between science and religion hardly became conspicuous until after *The*

Origin of Species and the Civil War, and for poets it does not seem at any time to have been so urgent a problem as it was in England. Poe, to be sure, could—some years after Keats's *Lamia*—declare science a vulture that preyed upon the poet's heart and drove hamadryads and naiads from wood and flood; later, Longfellow, Lowell, and Whittier, somewhat reassured by the religious solidity of Agassiz, hoped, in less romantic terms, that science might not kill divine mystery and reverence; and later still came the fervent affirmations of William Vaughn Moody; but New England Transcendentalism and new-world optimism cushioned Emerson, Thoreau, and Whitman against the fear of science.

For Emerson the poet, science may supply footnotes to the soul's intuitions, and its partial truths cannot be at odds with Truth. Since all life is one, since all nature and human experience are but aspects of universal Being, there is nothing to dread. Emerson's vision of 'the perfect whole' (though disturbed at times by the consciousness of slavery or of 'Things . . . in the saddle') leaves small room for doubt or evil or anything but serene acceptance of all that nature teaches and creative energy provides, including a Transcendentalized version of evolution.

Thoreau, who could see most men as leading lives of quiet desperation, had a clearer vision of actuality, a fuller sense of human weakness and the need of discipline, but he had also a large measure of the optimism which is proof against the facts of life. He did not, for instance, share Tennyson's and Keats's and many other men's revulsion against nature red in tooth and claw. Thoreau loved to see nature carried out in the fisherman who swallows the pickerel which swallows the perch which swallows the grub-worm—'and so all the chinks in the scale of being are filled.' And he loved to see nature so prodigally creative 'that myriads can be afforded to be sacrificed and suffered to prey on one another; that tender organizations can be so serenely squashed out of existence like pulp. . .' Thoreau was not, of course, so happily detached when he contemplated a mechanized civilization and the human struggle for survival and mundane success.

> Men say they know many things;
> But lo! they have taken wings,—
> The arts and sciences,
> And a thousand appliances:
> The wind that blows
> Is all that anybody knows.

As for the astronomical universe, Thoreau was no Pascal or Herbert Spencer. He recognized that the earth is but a point in space, yet 'why should I feel lonely? is not our planet in the Milky Way?' To be sure, he wasn't very far from Concord.

Walt Whitman sometimes echoes Emerson's Transcendental oracles, sometimes translates them into the particular terms of American expansion. He is intoxicated alike by the practical achievements of science and industry and by the infinities of time and space. The poet, if not the citizen, has an all-embracing confidence which sees no problems, no possible cause for doubt or dismay in the mundane or the cosmic situation, since all things declare and nourish the greatness of man's soul. Whitman has some affinity with Blake, but not in his jubilant view of factories and progress. His cosmic and evolutionary optimism may be illustrated by some bits from the *Song of Myself:*

Before I was born out of my mother generations guided me,
My embryo has never been torpid, nothing could overlay it.

For it the nebula cohered to an orb,
The long slow strata piled to rest it on,

Vast vegetables gave it sustenance,
Monstrous sauroids transported it in their mouths and deposited
    it with care.

All forces have been steadily employ'd to complete and delight me,
Now on this spot I stand with my robust soul. . .

I have said that the soul is not more than the body,
And I have said that the body is not more than the soul,
And nothing, not God, is greater to one than one's self is. . .

And I say to any man or woman, Let your soul stand cool and
    composed before a million universes. . .

In *Democratic Vistas* (1871) Whitman could still 'hail with
joy the oceanic, variegated, intense practical energy, the de-
mand for facts, even the business materialism of the current
age,' though his main text was 'woe to the age or land in
which these things, movements, stopping at themselves, do not
tend to ideas.' Business and science stride forward, while the
poetic and prophetic imagination lags far behind; literature
flourishes on the lowest level of entertainment, but the life of
the spirit is impoverished and corrupt. And Whitman calls
for literature, for poetry, worthy of the nation's past and
future, 'a literature underlying life, religious, consistent with
science, handling the elements and forces with competent
power, teaching and training men,' making 'sane and heroic'
the vast soulless body of society.

Among the many poets who were kindled by Whitman's
example and challenge, perhaps the most lineal and worship-
ful successor was Hart Crane, though Crane was also a kind
of modern Poe. His unhappy life ended with suicide in 1932.
In his most ambitious work, *The Bridge* (1930), Crane attempted an epic of America, a fusion of native myth with en-

gineering. Columbus (the conqueror of space), Pocahontas (the fertile American earth and its Indian past), Rip Van Winkle, Whitman (the prophet of America), the Mississippi, and the rough texture of common life were combined with Brooklyn Bridge, New York, subway and transcontinental trains, airplanes, and many other things. The poem was a heroic and grandiose effort to fuse machinery and the soul, to find spiritual unity in modern multiplicity, but its success was in some of its parts. The Bridge remains a half-inert frame for kaleidoscopic vignettes and visions, and as a whole the poem rather reflects than transcends chaos, both the outward chaos of its material and the inward chaos of a romantic and dubiously mystical sensibility excited by conceptions it cannot control.

If Crane in some measure carried on Whitman's optimism, nearly all other modern American poets have more or less repudiated it and have been preoccupied with the general predicament of modern man. One herald of the new spirit was Edwin Arlington Robinson, who, whether in Tilbury Town or Camelot, felt the atmospheric pressure of a skeptical age. Modern poets may or may not touch science directly, but, as I said, they are all conditioned by it, from the deceptively homespun Robert Frost, who has surveyed man and the cosmos with a stable Yankee fortitude and irony, to the deceptively elegant Marianne Moore, John Crowe Ransom, and Wallace Stevens, from the civic-minded Mr. MacLeish with his strain of heroic primitivism to Mr. Jeffers with his violently nihilistic primitivism—and many other poets of distinction or promise. But although modern American poets have turned away from the general optimism of the golden age to contemplate the human creature shivering in an inhuman world, they—or some of them—can still find a measure of positive happiness in living and in the American scene. Modern English poets have been, in comparison, much more immediately conscious of a broken if not ruined civilization; witness, for example, Edith Sitwell's *The Shadow of Cain*, a poem, by the way, in which modern science is mixed with echoes of Paracelsus, Donne, and Thomas Burnet's *Sacred Theory of the Earth*. In the last few years, however, there has arisen among the younger English poets a new romanticism or individualism which has had elements of personal and positive affirmation. But we are concerned with the half-century at large and we had better look at a few representative figures than try to catalogue or generalize about a great many.

First of all we must notice an elaborate work which in some respects stands apart from its age. In 1929 a long philosophic poem, Robert Bridges' *Testament of Beauty*, became a best seller, whether or not it was read by all the people who bought it. There was something impressive in the mere fact of such an affirmation from a man of 85, a poet, moreover, who had written beautifully as a cloistered and precious artist and had hitherto touched moral ideas in mainly decorative or lyrical terms. (Bridges had, to be sure, surveyed science and thought in two poems in classical prosody.) But the *Testament,* though it was the most ambitious successor to *In Memoriam* as a reconciling of evolution with the ethical dignity and destiny of man, can hardly sustain the parallel or remain an equivalent landmark in modern poetry. Tennyson had to conquer stark despair; Bridges did not. His ethical, religious, and aesthetic creed was an eclectic compound drawn from Plato (without Plato's dualism), Aristotle, Christianity, and modern philosophers and poets, but in the main it was an attempt to fuse naturalism and idealism by way of Santayana; and if Santayana was a partial Epicurus, Bridges was no Lucretius. A better analogy might be with Pope and Shaftesbury (or Bolingbroke). Bridges has a deeper wisdom and a higher vision than Pope, but he has perhaps no less philosophical inconsistency and certainly no less optimism. The facts of human nature seem too readily submissive to the harmonious moulds of ideal reason and beauty; Meredith's evolutionary doctrine, to which Bridges' bears some small resemblance, was more realistic. While there is no question of Bridges' desire to accept man as an evolving animal, or of the noble purity of his idealism, the reader, in approving much of the sermon, may find the poem a piece of aloof, archaic, and often beautiful unreality.

At the other end of the cultural scale from this aristocratic traditionalist was the miner's son, D. H. Lawrence. Lawrence's early evangelicalism gave way before Darwin and the rest, but not his craving for a religion. As T. S. Eliot said, his vision was spiritual, but spiritually sick; he was one of the last and most fevered embodiments of 'the romantic agony.' Lawrence had a complete hatred for intellect, science, and a mechanized civilization, which had blighted all that was mysterious and vital in life. There was much of the pathetic, and not a little of the grotesque, in his desperate efforts to escape into a primitive, unspoiled world, Italy, Ceylon, Australia, or New Mexico. Whereas Meredith glorified the disciplined harmony of blood, brain, and spirit, Lawrence abhorred the dry brain and glorified instinct and impulse. His creed embraced the glandular and the theosophical, the fleshly and the mythical. In his poetry, his intense preoccupation with animal energies enabled him to render physical sensation with extraordinary vividness, if we can respond very fully to such limited perceptions. In general, Lawrence's primitivistic vitalism was an earnest attempt, in the face of positivistic science, to reaffirm what he believed to be the religious sources of life and faith.

W. B. Yeats, a more complex nature than Lawrence and a far greater poet, arrived at a partly similar position. He had little to say of science in his poetry, but his whole evolution and his whole body of writing were, like Lawrence's, a kind of answer to it. Yeats also belonged to the generations that were deprived of traditional religious faith by Darwin and Tyndall, and for a long time his romantic idealism found the beauty it craved in the ivory tower; but he was strong enough to make his way out again, by labyrinthine passages. To use his own metaphor, he made himself a coat embroidered out of old mythologies, but, when fools caught and wore it, he found there was more enterprise in going naked. Unable to achieve spiritual unity by orthodox roads, religious or rational, or to gather from Celtic romance a myth adequate for the modern mind, Yeats explored various and dubious mystical and occult tunnels. One of his revivifying sources is of special interest to us, the conception of the *Anima Mundi* that he met in Henry More, the Cambridge Platonist and opponent of Descartes and Hobbes. Yeats came to recognize, like his beloved Blake and like Coleridge, that the trouble had begun with the mechanistic materialism of More's age and had been growing steadily worse. What he, as a poet, desired was a world to be contemplated, not a world to be conquered and remade by Baconian science. I might quote from Yeats what is certainly the shortest and perhaps not the least comprehensive history of modern civilization:

> Locke sank into a swoon;
> The Garden died;
> God took the spinning-jenny
> Out of his side.*

*'Fragments,' *Collected Poems* by W. B. Yeats (copyright, 1933, by The Macmillan Company; renewed, 1961, by Bertha Georgie Yeats). Used by permission of The Macmillan Company, Mr. M. B. Yeats, the Macmillan Co. of Canada, and Macmillan & Co., Ltd.

In the poems of his late maturity, when he had in some sense attained his goal—but still with the tensions of unresolved conflicts—and when he had completely mastered the art of walking naked, Yeats could respond to two visions or ideals which are, roughly, the alternatives of all art. One of these visions or ideals moves, in Yeats's poetry, on several planes. There is such an impassioned fusion of the animal, the human, and the divine as *Leda and the Swan*. There is the quieter contemplation of the harmonious unity of man's vital energies and the universe, as in the familiar lines which may remind us of Emerson's *Brahma*:

> O chestnut tree, great rooted blossomer,
> Are you the leaf, the blossom or the bole?
> O body swayed to music, O brightening glance,
> How can we know the dancer from the dance? *

Then there are the poems in which old age regrets passing time and the withering of vitality and calls up the memory of lovely women and bold men. On a lower level of naturalism, and of poetry, are the salty pieces that glorify sensual participation rather than contemplation (these have no parallels in Emerson).

If one labels many of Yeats's best poems naturalistic (in a crude classification that ignores their complexity and intensity), it is partly in order to define the character of the other vision or ideal. For in such a great poem as *Sailing to Byzantium*, a poet who is often disposed to mock Plotinus and cry in Plato's teeth turns away from the Many to the One. The resolution is aesthetic rather than religious, and represents only moments of vision, but it is a resolution, the statement

*'Among School Children,' *Collected Poems* by W. B. Yeats (copyright, 1928, by The Macmillan Company; renewed, 1956, by Georgie Yeats). Used by permission of The Macmillan Company, Mr. M. B. Yeats, the Macmillan Co. of Canada, and Macmillan & Co., Ltd.

of an idealism based on full recognition of the power of nature's 'sensual music.'

A very different resolution has been arrived at by the last poet we can consider, Mr. Eliot. The first hints of *The Waste Land* appeared in early sketches of the drab, dismal monotony of urban life; and in other early poems appeared the flashback technique, the contrasts between ideal heroic past and decayed squalid present (not without suggestions that such a past is illusory). So far as Mr. Eliot did find spiritual health in another age, his backward glances were much the same in intent, if not in manner, as Arnold's visions of 'The freshness of the early world.' From the beginning also Mr. Eliot could both use old and create new myths and symbolic figures, from apeneck Sweeney, the embodiment of gross, unthinking, animal lusts and satisfactions, to J. Alfred Prufrock, the timid, introspective suburbanite who is no Tristram or Lancelot and cannot hearken to the sirens' call to freedom and fulfilment. The poet's awareness of science was conveyed, like everything else, obliquely. In *Sweeney among the Nightingales* the human derelicts, in a tavern near the Convent of the Sacred Heart, are presented in animal terms, and in *Whispers of Immortality* Grishkin's friendly bust 'Gives promise of pneumatic bliss.'

In *The Waste Land* (1922) the complex symbolism, derived from *The Golden Bough,* the Grail romances, and other sources, sets up perpetual contrasts between spiritual health and a mechanized, neurotic, Godless civilization that is dry and sterile:

> What are the roots that clutch, what branches grow
> Out of this stony rubbish? Son of man,
> You cannot say, or guess, for you know only
> A heap of broken images, where the sun beats,

> And the dead tree gives no shelter, the cricket no relief,
> And the dry stone no sound of water.*

The elliptical, discontinuous technique of the poem mirrors, rather too directly, the isolated, fragmentary, meaningless existences it describes. The main area of experience drawn upon is that of sex, since it has been so dominant in the modern mind and provides such signal variations on the main theme. In the world of mass-production and the assembly-line, the individual has lost his traditional roots and vision, and even love has become biological mechanics. The burden of this poem is that freedom and fulfilment are found, not in heeding the sirens' sensual song, but in religious faith and self-abnegation.

The Waste Land was among other things one of those poems that fix the spirit of an age before the age has become conscious of itself. It was at first taken to be the very voice and monument of postwar defeatism, of the lost generation and the hollow men, the picture of a dying Europe. It was that in part, but it might rather be called the *Inferno* of Mr. Eliot's *Divine Comedy*. In his later poetry the religious theme has deepened, and narrowed, in a sense, to something like exclusion of the concrete world. The subject of *Four Quartets* is man's religious redemption from the flux of time and circumstance. If the poet conceives the old and central problem of sinful man in terms of an old religion, he can also combine

*T. S. Eliot: *Collected Poems 1909-1962* (Copyright, 1936, by Harcourt, Brace & World, Inc.; copyright, 1963, 1964, by T. S. Eliot). Used by permission of Harcourt, Brace & World, Inc., and Faber and Faber, Ltd.

The 'heap of broken images' may be an echo of Tennyson's *Two Voices*:

> Heaven opens inward, chasms yawn,
> Vast images in glimmering dawn,
> Half shown, are broken and withdrawn.

those terms with images from modern science. The London
Underground, with its strained, time-ridden faces, becomes
our actual world, a Dantesque hell. And while airplanes—
which appeared a century ago in *Locksley Hall*—fly all
through modern poetry as symbols of scientific slaughter and
destruction, Mr. Eliot's use of the image is unique. The fire
from a bombing plane is fused with the fire of self-love or lust
and the fire of divine love:

> The dove descending breaks the air
> With flame of incandescent terror
> Of which the tongues declare
> The one discharge from sin and error.
> The only hope, or else despair
>   Lies in the choice of pyre or pyre—
>   To be redeemed from fire by fire.*

This sketch of science and English poetry began with the
theme of mutability and some early poets' religious visions of
release. With *Four Quartets*—which carries epigraphs from
Heraclitus—we may be said to have come full circle. Mr. Eliot,
like Spenser and Donne and others, sees man as a sinful being
compelled, in the world of nature, to seek the world of grace.
If his acceptance of a traditional faith has, in spite of his vast
literary influence, set him apart from contemporary liberal
minds, it is also true that he has had a large share in making
religion respected among intellectuals. And in that he is only
the chief poetic representative of a distinct movement of our
time. For the modern recognition of man's plight has led in
two opposed directions, to pleas for more science (and more
social science) and to a religious revival.

*'Little Gidding,' *Four Quartets* (Copyright, 1943, by T. S. Eliot). Used
by permission of Harcourt, Brace & World, Inc., and Faber and Faber, Ltd.

Among the one or two thousand recent scientific books there are not a few that urge science as the one remedy for all our ills, metaphysical, international, social, and individual. Some colleges have greatly enlarged their requirements in science— which suggests curing delirium tremens with brandy. The mass of scientists are no doubt humble men, rightly concerned with advancing human knowledge and welfare and hardly less disturbed than laymen and poets by the dangers of science mis-applied (though perhaps less aware of more insidious effects); and such scientists would not, it may be supposed, welcome the extravagant and even crassly barbarian claims made by some spokesmen for science and positivism. At the same time scientists in general are not inclined to accept any faith that goes beyond the demonstrated facts and hypotheses of science.

For the religious revival, one might refer to the vogue of the nineteenth-century Kierkegaard and to such various modern names as von Hügel (whom Yeats dismissed, though with a blessing), Berdyaev, Kafka, Maritain, du Noüy, Niebuhr, Toynbee, Charles Williams, Eliot, and Auden, or to the wide popularity of C. S. Lewis' religious books and religio-scientific fables. We can observe a phenomenon which would have been inconceivable twenty-five years ago, the currency, in the intellectual and critical vocabulary, of such words as 'guilt,' 'pride,' 'grace,' 'redemption,' 'God.' As some of these words and names suggest, this movement has been rather in the tradition of Augustine and Calvin than in the rational tradition of the old Christian humanism. In any case, although the men just named can scarcely be charged with lack of intelligence, they would signify, to good liberals, only an emotional and authoritarian escape from reason and scientific truth. It might be added that the charge of defective intelligence could still less be brought against the late Professor Whitehead, whose metaphysical doctrine had a religious, if quite undogmatic, foundation. If it be said that the religious revival has, among the literary, inspired some doubtful religiosity, it must be said that even religiosity is significant as evidence of a need that science cannot satisfy.

Whether or not a modern poet's outlook is religious (and a completely non-religious poet is almost a contradiction in terms), it is safe to affirm that poets in general have started from a conviction of the bankruptcy of the secular and scientific optimism which has been growing since the Renaissance. We have followed poetic revolts against scientific and mechanistic views of the world and man, and nowadays, when the odds are overwhelmingly heavy, most poets, I think, would accept Mr. Gerald Heard's historical summary (without necessarily accompanying him further):

Newton banished God from nature, Darwin banished him from life, Freud drove him from the last fastness, the soul. It was all latent in Newton, in Descartes, in Galileo: mechanism would conquer all, once it had conquered nature, for man's body was sprung from nature and his mind from his body.*

It may be of course that science does contain all truth, that religion in our day is only the lingering flush of a sun that has set, and that, as Mr. Richards argued in 1926, poetry will retain its saving power only if severed from belief, from the 'Magical View' of the world. But if that is the point we have arrived at, it may still be doubted whether such poetry could possess such power. For a number of modern writers, at any rate, original sin is a fact of experience, as thoroughly valid as any fact of the laboratory. That, if we think of the greatest

---

* *The Third Morality* (London: Cassell; New York: Morrow, 1937), p. 33 (in English edition); quoted by Geoffrey West, *Charles Darwin* (Routledge, 1937, p. 317; Yale University Press, 1938, p. 325).

writers of the past, is not quite enough, since we need faith in man's nobility also; but it means a considerably larger measure of spiritual health than trust in science and the social sciences as the one and the complete guide to life.

It has been said that men of religion tell many little lies for the sake of one big truth, while men of science tell many little truths for the sake of one big lie. The saying can be translated into terms less offensive to both parties, even if the terms are inevitably platitudinous. Physical science has a firm and expanding hold upon truth, but its truth is limited and partial; it assuredly cannot claim to be an explanation of ultimate reality, and it has little or no concern with the realm of value. So far as science goes, man can be defined as a conglomeration of chemicals or as 'an ape in an airplane.' It is sometimes argued that modern science, in moving beyond the tight dogmas of nineteenth-century science to recognition of the inexplicable, has come nearer to poetry, and that poetry and science are really sisters, or at least cousins, under the skin, because both seek the universal through study of the particular. None the less, the gulf remains very wide, as it is between science and religion. To quote Whitehead,

The fact of the religious vision, and its history of persistent expansion, is our one ground for optimism. Apart from it, human life is a flash of occasional enjoyments lighting up a mass of pain and misery, a bagatelle of transient experience.*

The poetic vision, like the religious, is of the inmost realities and the wholeness of individual experience in a mysterious world, and it works upon the individual. Whatever the varying motives and the varying adequacy of poets in this or that

* *Science and the Modern World* (copyright 1925 by The Macmillan Company). Used by permission.

period, the poetic apprehension of life has its own validity; and the essential function of poetry is to preserve, discipline, and enrich the humanity, humility, and spirituality of man in the midst of the dehumanizing forces that more and more envelop him.